MW01166961

www.wadsworth.com

wadsworth.com is the World Wide Web site for
Wadsworth and is your direct source to dozens of
online resources.

At *wadsworth.com* you can find out about
supplements, demonstration software, and
student resources. You can also send e-mail to
many of our authors and preview new publications
and exciting new technologies.

wadsworth.com
Changing the way the world learns®

IN BRIEF
A Handbook
for Writers

WADSWORTH DEVELOPMENTAL ENGLISH
BUILDING BRIDGES TO SUCCESS

New for 2000

WRITING

Rogers/Rogers, *Patterns and Themes: A Basic English Reader*, 4th ed.

Robinson/Tucker, *Texts and Contexts: A Contemporary Approach to College Writing*, 4th ed.

Tyner, *College Writing Basics: A Progressive Approach*, 5th ed.

McDonald/Salomone, *The Writer's Response: A Reading-Based Approach to College Writing*, 2nd ed.

READING

Maker/Lenier, *College Reading with the Active Critical Thinking Method, Book 1*, 5th ed.

Maker/Lenier, *College Reading with the Active Critical Thinking Method, Book 2*, 6th ed.

Sotiriou/Phillips, *Steps to Reading Proficiency*, 5th ed.

STUDY SKILLS

Van Blerkom, *College Study Skills: Becoming a Strategic Learner*, 3rd ed.

Other Developmental English Titles

WRITING

Richard-Amato, *World Views: Multicultural Literature for Critical Writers, Readers, and Thinkers* (1998)

Salomone/McDonald, *Inside Writing: A Writer's Workbook, Form A*, 4th ed. (1999)

Wingersky/Boerner/Holguin-Balogh, *Writing Paragraphs and Essays: Integrating Reading, Writing, and Grammar Skills*, 3rd ed. (1999)

READING

Atkinson/Longman, *Reading Enhancement and Development*, 6th ed. (1999)

Maker/Lenier, *Academic Reading with Active Critical Thinking* (1996)

STUDY SKILLS

Longman/Atkinson, *College Learning and Study Skills*, 5th ed. (1999)

Longman/Atkinson, *Study Methods and Reading Techniques*, 2nd ed. (1999)

Sotiriou, *Integrating College Study Skills: Reasoning in Reading, Listening, and Writing*, 5th ed. (1999)

Smith/Knudsvig/Walter, *Critical Thinking: Building the Basics* (1998)

INSTRUCTOR'S EDITION

IN BRIEF
A Handbook
for Writers

STEPHEN MCDONALD
Palomar College

WILLIAM SALOMONE
Palomar College

Wadsworth
Thomson Learning™

Australia • Canada • Denmark • Japan • Mexico • New Zealand •
Philippines • Puerto Rico • Singapore • South Africa • Spain •
United Kingdom • United States

Publisher: Karen J. Allanson
Sr. Development Editor: Kimberly Johnson
Sr. Editorial Assistant: Godwin Chu
Marketing Manager: Jennie Burger
Project Editor: Christal Niederer
Print Buyer: Barbara Britton

Permissions Editor: Susan Walters
Production: Johnstone Associates
Designer: Adriane Bosworth
Cover Design: Bill Stanton
Compositor: G & S Typesetters, Inc.
Printer: Malloy Lithographing, Inc.

For permission to use material from this text,
contact us by
    web: www.thomsonrights.com
    fax: 1-800-730-2215
    phone: 1-800-730-2214

Wadsworth / Thomson Learning
10 Davis Drive
Belmont, CA 94002-3098
USA
www.wadsworth.com

International Headquarters
Thomson Learning
290 Harbor Drive, 2nd Floor
Stamford, CT 06902-7477
USA

UK/Europe/Middle East
Thomson Learning
Berkshire House
168-173 High Holborn
London WC1V 7AA
United Kingdom

Asia
Thomson Learning
60 Albert Street #15-01
Albert Complex
Singapore 189969

Canada
Nelson/Thomson Learning
1120 Birchmount Road
Scarborough, Ontario M1K 5G4
Canada

Library of Congress
Cataloging-in-Publication Data
McDonald, Stephen
    In Brief : a handbook for writers / Stephen
McDonald, William Salomone.
        p.   cm.
    Includes index.
    ISBN 0-534-52408-7
    1. English language—Rhetoric Handbooks,
manuals, etc.   2. English language—
Grammar Handbooks, manuals, etc.
    3. Report writing Handbooks, manuals, etc.
    I. Salomone, William.   II. Title.
PE1408.M3945   2000
808'.042—dc21   99-32492
Instructor's Edition: 0-534-52409-5

For Marste, Jenna, and Chelsea

Contents

PART 1 ❖ WRITING THE FORMAL PAPER   1

Finding Your Ideas   3

Recognizing the Shape of a Paper   7

Writing a Thesis Statement   10

Organizing Your Points   13

Writing an Introductory Paragraph   16

Opening Each Body Paragraph with a Topic Sentence   20

Developing Your Body Paragraphs with Supporting Sentences   22

Writing a Concluding Paragraph   25

Revising the Paper   27

Editing and Proofreading the Paper   30

Formatting the Paper   32

Composing on a Computer   35

PART 2 ❖ SPECIAL ASSIGNMENTS   37

The In-Class Paper and Essay Examination   39

Reading Actively and Accurately   42

Writing a Summary   46

The Research Paper   48

Documentating Your Sources   55

Sample Research Paper   61

PART 3 ❖ EDITING YOUR PAPERS   67

Sentences

Complete Sentences   69
   Exercise 71

x   ◆   CONTENTS

Sentence Fragments   72
Exercise 74

Run-on Sentences   75
Exercise 76

Verbs

Subject-Verb Agreement   78
Exercise 80

Consistency in Verb Tense   82
Exercise 83

Consistency in Verb Voice   84
Exercise 86

Pronouns

Pronoun Agreement   87
Exercise 89

Pronoun Reference   90
Exercise 91

Pronoun Case   92
Exercise 94

Modifiers

Misplaced Modifiers   96
Exercise 97

Dangling Modifiers   98
Exercise 99

Punctuation

Commas   101
Exercise 104

Semicolons   105
Exercise 106

Colons   108
Exercise 108

Apostrophes   110
Exercise 111

Quotation Marks   112
Exercise 114

Mechanics

Titles   115
  Exercise 116

Capitalization   117
  Exercise 118

Numbers   119
  Exercise 120

Word Choice and Spelling

Commonly Confused Words   121
  Exercise 126

Spelling Rules   127
  Exercise 129

PART 4 ❖ ESL CONCERNS   131

Using *A, An,* or *The*   133
  Exercise 134

Using Helping Verbs and Main Verbs   135
  Exercise 137

Placing Adjectives Correctly and Using Participles
  as Adjectives   138
  Exercise 139

PART 5 ❖ WRITING WITH STYLE   141

Not Too Formal—Not Too Informal   143
  Exercise 144

Avoiding Clichés and Euphemisms   146
  Exercise 148

Cutting Excess Words   149
  Exercise 151

Using Parallel Sentence Structure   153
  Exercise 154

Varying Sentence Length and Structure   155
  Exercise 157

APPENDIX ❖ ANSWERS TO
ODD-NUMBERED EXERCISES   159

INDEX ❖   167

PREFACE

The Reason for This Text

We have written *In Brief* in response to the need for a simple, concise, friendly handbook, one that will not overwhelm students as it covers the basics of writing a paper. In it we offer brief, easy-to-follow chapters on writing college essays, summaries, research papers, and essay exams. We provide instruction in editing and proofreading for errors in grammar, mechanics, and punctuation. We discuss common ESL problems, and we briefly cover stylistic concerns such as avoiding clichés, cutting needless words, and using parallelism and sentence variety. Our goal throughout the text has been to present this material as clearly and concisely as possible. We want beginning writers to feel confident that they can open this text to any chapter and find advice they can understand and use.

In *Brief* can be used for a number of purposes. It provides the instructor who wants to teach developmental classes without a full rhetoric or handbook the means to do so. At the same time, it provides a supplement for instructors whose primary text does not include instruction in the writing of essays and basic research papers or in the rules of grammar, mechanics, and punctuation. It also can be used by instructors outside of the English Department, particularly those who require papers and reports but whose students have not yet taken freshman English.

Organization

We have organized *In Brief* so that it moves from larger writing concerns ("Writing the Formal Paper" and "Special Assignments") to more specific concerns ("Editing Your Papers" and "ESL Concerns"), ending with a section on "Writing with Style." Our philosophy implicit in this organization is that students need help first with generating, arranging, and presenting ideas, and only later with the editing of grammar, punctuation, and spelling.

Part 1: Writing the Formal Paper

We all know that students want clear directions and definite rules, but we also know that writing is a recursive, often messy, process. Part 1 presents students with clear steps to follow when writing a formal paper while still acknowledging the creative, roundabout nature of writing. It opens with a discussion of prewriting techniques ("Finding Your Ideas") and then moves through a step-by-step discussion of the elements of a successful essay, explaining how to develop a thesis statement from the prewriting material, how to organize ideas to support the thesis statement, and how to write an introductory paragraph that concludes with the thesis. It then discusses topic sentences, paragraph development, concluding paragraphs, and revision techniques, ending with instruction on "Formatting the Paper" and "Composing on the Computer."

Part 2: Special Assignments

Part 2 is designed to help students with specific concerns about writing in-class papers, essay examinations, summaries, and research papers. It also presents instruction in reading and annotating texts. The section on the research paper covers areas such as finding and limiting a topic, doing the research, using computerized databases as well as the Internet, taking notes, organizing ideas, and integrating quotations and paraphrases. "Documenting Your Sources" discusses how to use MLA guidelines to write parenthetical references and a "Works Cited" page. Finally, Part 2 presents an annotated sample research paper.

Part 3: Editing Your Papers

This section presents brief, easy-to-follow chapters on the basics of grammar, punctuation, mechanics, and spelling. Each chapter ends with a ten-sentence exercise, with answers to the odd-numbered sentences in the appendix.

Part 4: ESL Concerns

Part 4 offers instruction for non-native speakers of English in several particularly troublesome areas: the use of *a, an,* and *the,* the use of helping verbs and main verbs, the placement of adjectives, and the use of participles as adjectives. Each chapter ends with a ten-sentence exercise, with answers to the odd-numbered sentences in the appendix.

Part 5: Writing with Style

This section offers five chapters designed to help students improve their style of writing, ranging from instruction in the appropriate level of vocabulary for college writing, to avoiding clichés and euphemisms, to cutting excess words, to using parallel sentence structure, to varying sentence length and structure. Each of these chapters also ends with a ten-sentence exercise, with answers to the odd-numbered sentences in the appendix.

Key Features

- The friendly, non-threatening tone, clear organization, and concise explanations make the text accessible to the beginning writer.

- Writing instruction, presented first, is followed by grammar and editing issues, emphasizing that the generation and arrangement of ideas precede the correction of errors.
- Separate chapters on "Reading Actively and Accurately" and "Writing a Summary" provide instruction in effective reading, annotating, and summarizing.
- Two chapters, "The Research Paper" and "Documenting Your Sources," discuss the writing of a research paper, including how to conduct the research, take notes, and use MLA form for parenthetical documentation and the Works Cited page.
- A thorough discussion of the use of computers, databases, and the Internet brings students up to date with the latest technology available for use in research.
- A separate chapter presents a full-length sample research paper, allowing students to learn by example.
- Broad coverage of common problems in grammar, punctuation, spelling, and mechanics allows students to study areas of concern in their writing.
- A separate section on ESL issues assists non-native speakers.
- A separate section on "Writing with Style" allows instructors to move their classes beyond the basics.
- Short exercises at the end of each chapter in the "Editing," "ESL," and "Style" sections and answers to the odd-numbered exercises in the appendix provide students with a quick, in-text check of their comprehension.

Electronic and Online Supplements

- **Web Site.** Visit Wadsworth's Developmental English web site at http://devenglish.wadsworth.com. Here you will find many online teaching and learning aids.
- **Internet Trifold for Developmental English** (0-534-54744-3). This handy guide shows your students where to find online reading and writing resources. Package this trifold card with any Wadsworth Developmental English text for a very small cost. Contact your local Wadsworth representative for more information.

- **InfoTrac College Edition®.** This fully searchable, online database with access to full-text articles from over 900 periodicals provides a great resource for additional readings and/or research. Now available free when packaged with this text, InfoTrac College Edition offers authoritative sources, updated daily and going back as far as four years. Both you and your students can receive unlimited online use for one academic term. (Please contact your Thomson Learning representative for policy, pricing, and availability; international and school distribution is restricted. To order bundled with the text, use ISBN 0-534-75632-8.)

- **Custom Publishing.** You can combine your choice of chapters from specific Wadsworth titles with your own materials in a custom-bound book. To place your order, call the Thomson Learning Custom Order Center at 1 (800) 355-9983.

- **Videos.** Wadsworth has many videos available to qualifying adopters on topics such as improving your grades, notetaking practice, diversity, and many more. Contact your local Wadsworth representative for more information.

Acknowledgments

We wish to express our gratitude to the family members and friends who have encouraged and supported us during the writing of *In Brief,* as well as to our colleagues at Palomar College, whose advice and direction have influenced us and improved our teaching and writing in more ways than we can count.

We also extend our thanks to the many professionals at Wadsworth who have kept the wheels running so smoothly during the production of this text. Our special thanks go to Karen J. Allanson, publisher; Kim Johnson, senior development editor; Christal Niederer, project editor; Godwin Chu, senior editorial assistant; Jess McFadden, marketing assistant; and Judy Johnstone, who managed production from manuscript to printer.

Reviewers

Finally, we are grateful to the following professors who took their time to provide valuable input for this text:

Alan Ainsworth, Houston Community College
Jean Bernard, Bunker Hill Community College
Tracy Carrick, San Francisco State University
Claire Conrey, University of Massachusetts, Boston
David Elias, Eastern Kentucky University
Wambui Githiora-Updike, Roxbury Community College
Jefferson Hancock, West Valley College and Cabrillo College
Deanne Harper, Northeastern University
Fran Lozano, Gavilan College
Donald Mengay, Baruch College, City University of New York

Melissa Mentzer, Central Connecticut State University
Ferkins Reed, Urban Scholars Program, University of Massachusetts, Boston
Steve Straight, Manchester Community Technical College
Jonathan Taylor, Ferris State University
Marion Van Nostrand, Northeastern University
Karen Warren, Gavilan College

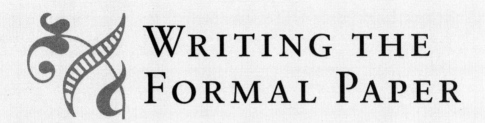

PART 1

WRITING THE FORMAL PAPER

FINDING YOUR IDEAS

RECOGNIZING THE SHAPE OF A PAPER

WRITING A THESIS STATEMENT

ORGANIZING YOUR POINTS

WRITING AN INTRODUCTORY PARAGRAPH

OPENING EACH BODY PARAGRAPH
WITH A TOPIC SENTENCE

DEVELOPING YOUR BODY PARAGRAPHS
WITH SUPPORTING SENTENCES

WRITING A CONCLUDING PARAGRAPH

REVISING THE PAPER

EDITING AND PROOFREADING THE PAPER

FORMATTING THE PAPER

COMPOSING ON A COMPUTER

Finding Your Ideas

We are all writers, after all. And whether we are beginners or professionals, we all face the same tasks. How do we begin to fill that empty paper or screen with words? How do we move from not writing to writing? And where do we find ideas that will be worth writing? There are as many answers to these questions as there are writers, but some techniques for getting started and finding ideas seem to work for almost everyone.

Getting Started? Try These Techniques

Freewriting

- Freewriting is exactly what its name suggests: writing *freely*, without censoring your thoughts or correcting grammar, spelling, or punctuation. To freewrite, type or write whatever you are thinking, whether or not it is related to your assignment. Pretend that you can't think without writing, that your hand writes whatever you think. Don't correct spelling, grammar, or punctuation. Just keep writing.

- If you are thinking about the amount of work that you have to do, write that down. If you don't know what topic to write about, write that down.

  I don't know what to write about. I wonder what a good topic would be for this paper. Maybe I could. . .

- Don't worry if your mind wanders from idea to idea. Just write down whatever enters your mind. The key is to start writing and to keep writing.

- After a few minutes, take a break and read what you have written. Look for a major idea that you might use as a paper topic. Then take that idea and freewrite about it, recording anything that comes to your mind about that topic. If unrelated thoughts creep in, record them too. Just keep writing without correcting any errors.

After ten or fifteen minutes of freewriting, you will have accomplished two things. First, you will have conquered writer's block because you have gotten out of the mode of merely *thinking* and into the mode of *writing as you think*. Second, you will have generated some ideas that you can use to develop into a more formal paper.

Brainstorming

- Brainstorming is another effective way to get started. It consists of making lists of ideas, usually in the form of words or phrases, not full sentences. Use brainstorming to find a topic for your paper by jotting down as many ideas you can.

- After a few minutes, review your list to see which topic interests you the most. If you still haven't found a good one, try alternating between freewriting and brainstorming. The trick is to keep writing, pausing every few minutes to review your material.

- If you already know what your paper topic will be, use brainstorming to make a list of ideas that you should include in your paper. Don't number your ideas or try to organize them yet. Just list whatever comes to mind, anything that might be included somewhere in your paper.

- Once you have a good list, group ideas that are related. Put a *1* before all ideas or details that would belong to one group, a *2* before those that would belong to a different group, and so on. Cross out ideas that you don't need. Then organize the groups so that they follow each other in a logical way.

- Once you have organized your ideas into groups, you can usually tell if you have enough material for a paper. If you don't, continue with freewriting and brainstorming to find more material to include.

Clustering

- Clustering is a writing technique that provides you with a picture of your thinking process. Write a possible topic in the middle of your page and draw a circle around it. Then connect any ideas or details that seem related to that idea, circling each idea and drawing a line to the original topic. Continue to connect new ideas as they occur to you.

- As in freewriting and brainstorming, allow your thoughts to flow freely. Write whatever occurs to you for ten or fifteen minutes. Then review what you have written to find the ideas that you could use in a paper. In the following example on the topic of "family relationships," the number of ideas under "divorce" suggests that the writer should focus on that topic.

Talking to Other People

Talking to other people can help to clarify your thoughts on a topic, especially if you keep the conversation focused on the assignment. Try telling someone

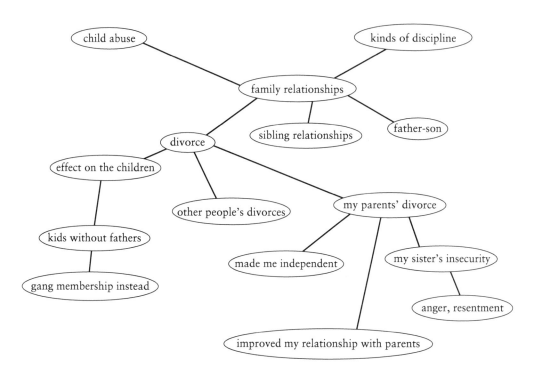

else what topics you are considering for your paper. Or, if you have already decided on a topic, tell someone what you intend to say about it and how you plan to organize your ideas. But be careful. Remember that talking is *not* writing. As soon as possible after your conversation, sit down and start to write.

MORE SUGGESTIONS FOR GETTING STARTED

Fill That Empty Page with Words

We all need to sit quietly and think about the topic sometimes, but try to do most of your thinking *in ink*. Remember, your job is to write a paper, not *think* a paper, so the sooner you start to write, the better off you'll be.

Worry About the Introduction Some Other Time

Many people write an introduction, tear it up and throw it away, and then write another one, tear it up and throw it away, and still another one, tear it up and throw it away, and so on for page after page of introductions. The problem is that they are trying to write their paper before they have done the initial work of freewriting, brainstorming, or clustering to generate ideas. Think about it. How can you introduce something that doesn't yet exist?

To avoid wasting hours trying to get past the first paragraph, spend your time writing down the ideas that you will cover in the paper. Forget about the introduction until you have decided upon the content of the paper.

Organize Your Ideas Later, Not Now

While brainstorming or freewriting, don't worry about the order of your points when you first write them down. In fact, if you are making a list of possible points to cover, don't even number them at first. For now, you should not be concerned about what will appear first or second or third. Instead, just write down whatever might appear *anywhere* in the paper. It doesn't matter if you list the eighth point first or the second point fifth. You just want to get down the ideas. You can organize them later.

Just for the Moment, Ignore Grammar, Spelling, and Punctuation

Yes, grammar, spelling, and punctuation are important. And, yes, they *must* be correct and accurate in college papers. But now is not the time to think about them. When you are getting started, you need to think about content, not mechanics. Remember, *to freewrite* means *to write freely*, so if you write *divorse* instead of *divorce* as you freewrite or brainstorm or cluster, don't worry about it. Just keep going. Get your ideas down. You'll edit the paper later.

Recognizing the Shape of a Paper

Most Papers Consist of an Introduction, Several Body Paragraphs, and a Conclusion

The length of the paper often determines the length and number of body paragraphs. There is no "rule" for how long or short to make a paragraph, but most 1,000-word college papers consist of three to five body paragraphs as well as an introduction and conclusion. A 500-word paper might include two or three body paragraphs, and a 2,000-word paper might use six to ten body paragraphs.

For the Most Part, Write Paragraphs That Are Relatively Similar in Length

There are many exceptions, but *in general* the paragraphs in your paper should present a balanced appearance. If you do have paragraphs that are quite different in length, one way to arrange them is to present the less developed paragraphs first, building up to the longer, more developed paragraphs.

Strengthen Short, Choppy Paragraphs

Short paragraphs (those with only two or three sentences) usually signal a need for more facts, examples, details, and explanations. (See the chapter "Developing Your Body Paragraphs with Supporting Sentences.") Sometimes a string of short paragraphs should simply be combined, especially if they are separate examples of the same idea.

Condense or Subdivide Excessively Long Paragraphs

Rarely will paragraphs in college papers be over one page long. Depending on the length of the entire paper, most of your paragraphs should be one-half to three-fourths of a typed, double-spaced page. That's about 150 to 250 words long. If one of your paragraphs is substantially longer than the others, you might need to rewrite it to condense its ideas. In addition, excessively long paragraphs can sometimes be subdivided as two separate paragraphs.

The Shape of a Brief Paper

Following is a diagram of a sample paper. The chapters explain the references to thesis statements, topic sentences, and supporting sentences.

Introductory Paragraph

Introductory Sentences	*See the chapter "Writing an Introductory Paragraph" for many ways to open an essay. Here are a few:* *A movement from general to specific statements* *An opening anecdote* *An opening quotation*
Thesis Statement	*Presents the main idea of the essay. See the chapter "Writing a Thesis Statement."*

First Body Paragraph

Topic Sentence	*Presents the main idea of the paragraph. See the chapter "Opening Each Body Paragraph with a Topic Sentence."*
Specific Support and Explanation	*See the chapter "Developing Your Body Paragraphs with Supporting Sentences."*
Specific Support and Explanation	*See the chapter "Developing Your Body Paragraphs . . ."*

Second Body Paragraph

Topic Sentence	*Presents the main idea of the paragraph. See the chapter "Opening Each Body Paragraph with a Topic Sentence."*
Specific Support and Explanation	*See the chapter "Developing Your Body Paragraphs with Supporting Sentences."*
Specific Support and Explanation	*See the chapter "Developing Your Body Paragraphs . . ."*

Third Body Paragraph

Topic Sentence	*Presents the main idea of the paragraph. See the chapter "Opening Each Body Paragraph with a Topic Sentence."*
Specific Support and Explanation	*See the chapter "Developing Your Body Paragraphs with Supporting Sentences."*
Specific Support and Explanation	*See the chapter "Developing Your Body Paragraphs . . ."*

Concluding Paragraph

Concluding Sentences	*See the chapter "Writing a Concluding Paragraph" for a variety of ways to close your essay. Here are a few:* *A restatement of the thesis idea* *A summary of the supporting points* *A prediction or recommendation* *A solution* *A quotation* *A reference to an anecdote from the introduction*

WRITING A THESIS STATEMENT

Write a Preliminary Thesis Statement

A thesis statement expresses the point of your paper in one or two sentences. Because it identifies the main idea of your paper, it is important that it be clear and accurate. Most thesis statements should appear in the last one or two sentences of your introductory paragraph and should be written as an assertion or statement, not as a question.

It is easy to write a thesis statement that is too vague and general or that doesn't really state your paper's point accurately. So think of your first thesis statement as a *preliminary* one. As you write your paper, plan on changing the thesis so that it accurately reflects what you are writing.

In Argumentative Papers, the Thesis Asserts an Opinion

Many college assignments will ask you to argue a controversial point. Should English be the official language of the United States? Should welfare programs be changed? Should gun ownership be restricted? Usually you will research topics like these, and the position you decide to take will be expressed in a thesis statement that asserts an opinion:

> *Declaring English the official language of the United States will create many more problems than it will solve.*

This thesis statement clearly states an opinion that needs to be supported with evidence. The body of this paper will now present supporting arguments, facts, and details to try to prove the opinion that declaring English the official language of the United States would create more problems than it would solve.

In Expository Papers, the Thesis Makes a Statement That Requires Explanation

Expository writing explains, analyzes, and categorizes rather than argues. An expository essay for a history class might explain why the South lost the Civil War. One for a geology class might analyze the different types of rock formations found in the Arizona deserts. And an expository essay for a sociology class might categorize different types of alcoholics. Thesis statements for expository papers need to identify the idea that the paper will explain:

> *The South lost the Civil War for economic, political, and military reasons.*

The Arizona deserts contain many fascinating rock formations.

Although all alcoholics suffer from a mental and physical dependence upon alcohol, there are different types of practicing alcoholics.

Note that each of the above thesis statements is focused on a specific topic that requires further explanation.

Sometimes a Thesis Should List the Supporting Points to Be Covered in the Paper

Many instructors prefer that your thesis list the supporting points that your paper will include. Since there is no "rule" here, ask your instructor which style he or she prefers. Here are two examples.

Argumentative thesis with supporting points included:

We should abolish the death penalty because it favors the rich over the poor, because it is applied in a discriminatory fashion, and because it sometimes results in the death of an innocent person.

Expository thesis with supporting points included:

Although all alcoholics suffer from a mental and physical dependence upon alcohol, there are different types of practicing alcoholics: the low-bottom drunk who has lost everything, the daily drinker who is still in denial, and the functional alcoholic who has yet to suffer the consequences of his disease.

Each of the above thesis statements identifies three points that the paper will cover.

Limit Your Thesis Statement to One Sentence

The thesis statement is like a road sign. A good one uses just a few words to identify exactly what lies ahead. So try to state your thesis in one sentence. If you have trouble doing so as you write your first draft, don't let that stop you from writing. Get your paper written. Once you have written your first draft, you should be able to return to your preliminary thesis and write it in only one sentence.

Place the Thesis Statement at the End of the Introduction

We'll discuss introductions later in Part 1, but in most college papers you should end the introductory paragraph with your thesis statement. (See the diagram of the first paragraph of a paper on page 8.)

Many types of writing outside of college papers place thesis statements in all sorts of places. Some don't even use formal thesis statements. But whenever clarity is most important, as it is in college essays, it is a good idea to place the thesis carefully and clearly at the end of the introduction.

Revise the Thesis Statement After You Have Written the First Draft

Until you have written a full draft of your paper, you are really working with a *preliminary* thesis statement. Your first attempt at a thesis identifies what you *think* you will write. But since you haven't actually written the paper yet, it's often difficult to express its main idea very well.

Things are different once you have written a complete first draft. Now you know what you have written, so now you can express the paper's main idea much more clearly and precisely. Go back to that preliminary thesis and improve it. One way to improve it is to look at the last paragraph of your draft. If you are like most writers, you have stated the main idea of your entire paper in that last paragraph much more clearly than you did in your preliminary thesis. So take that sentence from your last paragraph, improve it if it needs improving, and use it for your thesis.

Organizing Your Points

Be Sure You Have Enough Material

Before you organize your ideas, you need to decide what points your paper will cover. If you haven't made that decision yet, go back to the previous chapters and keep freewriting and brainstorming, or, if your paper involves research, continue with your outside reading and notetaking until you are relatively sure you have enough material for your paper.

How much is "enough"? That depends upon the required length and the purpose of the assignment. You need to gather enough material to meet any length requirements, but you also need enough to explain your ideas completely and clearly or, if you are arguing a point, to convince the reader of your position. In general, you are safer to develop too many points. You can always cut back if you need to.

Group Related Points

Once you know what points you will cover, review them to determine which ones are related and should be discussed together. Watch for specific examples, statistics, or quotations that should be grouped because they all illustrate the same point.

Set up a Tentative Organization

Arrange your points in whatever way seems most logical.

❖ **Spatial Order**

A spatial organization is used when you need to describe a place or object. In general, try to organize such a description so it follows the order in which one might actually observe the place or object. For instance, an observer would probably notice the larger elements of a place or the overall shape of an object before noticing any of the minor details.

❖ **Chronological Order**

Chronological order presents material as it actually happened. Whatever happened first is discussed first, whatever came second is discussed second, and so on. This organization is effective if your paper is describing an event, explaining how something happened, or giving instructions.

❖ **Emphatic Order**

Use this order to indicate a change in emphasis as your paper moves from one point to the next. Papers using this order usually move from the simplest or least difficult points to the most complex or most difficult ones. Here are some common patterns:

• Weakest point to strongest point
• Least dramatic point to most dramatic point
• Simplest point to most complex point

Notice that each of these patterns saves the point that will require the most explanation to the last (the strongest, most dramatic, and most complex points). Patterns like these create a sense of increasing importance as your paper progresses.

❖ **Comparison/Contrast Order**

Many college assignments will ask you to analyze the differences and/or the similarities between two topics. Here are two possible organizations for such an assignment, using as an example a comparison/contrast of the effects of cigarettes and alcohol.

• Point-by-Point

    I. Introduction
   II. First point: Effects upon the body
      A. cigarettes
      B. alcohol
  III. Second point: Effects upon mental attitude
      A. cigarettes
      B. alcohol
  IV. Third point: Effects upon others
      A. cigarettes
      B. alcohol
     (more points as needed)
   V. Conclusion

• Parallel Order

    I. Introduction
   II. First point: Effects of cigarettes upon the body
  III. Second point: Effects of cigarettes upon mental attitude

IV. Third point: Effects of cigarettes upon others
    (more points as needed)

 V. First point: Effects of alcohol upon the body

VI. Second point: Effects of alcohol upon mental attitude

VII. Third point: Effects of alcohol upon others
    (more points as needed)

 V. Conclusion

Of the two organizations listed above, the point-by-point order is most common in college writing because it keeps the two topics, A and B, closely related, discussing each point in terms of A and B before moving to the next point.

Sometimes a paper won't seem to fit any of these organizations. In that case, arrange your points in whatever way makes the most sense to you. If, for example, you are asked to write a paper defining a problem and proposing a solution to it, you might have to write three or more paragraphs using chronological order to explain how the problem came about. Then you might use emphatic order for several paragraphs to explain how the problem should be resolved, moving from the least significant to the most significant solution.

Allow Your Organization to Change as You Write Your Paper

Nothing is set in concrete at this point. When you begin to write your paper, do not be surprised if you think you should change the tentative organization you have decided upon. Remember, writing is a creative process. Some of your best ideas will come halfway through your first draft, no matter how well you have planned the paper.

Writing an Introductory Paragraph

The Purpose of an Introduction

The introduction to a college paper has two primary functions: to introduce the topic and to identify the thesis of the paper. Of course, an introduction can serve many other functions in addition to these two. It can capture the reader's interest, give some background information, establish the tone (serious, informal, humorous) of the paper. But regardless of these other functions, your introduction in college writing must succeed in clearly introducing the topic and identifying the thesis. If you keep these two objectives in mind, you will write successful introductions.

Write a Preliminary Introduction

- Do *not* let the introductory paragraph prevent you from writing the first draft of your paper. If you find yourself throwing out one sheet of paper after another because you can't write a good introduction, quit trying to write a *good* one. Instead, write a preliminary introduction.

- A preliminary introduction is one that you will more than likely not use because it is so rough, but at least it gets you going. You can write something as simplistic as this: *This is my introduction for my paper about attitudes toward homeless people.* Then write your preliminary thesis: *Attitudes toward homeless people seem to vary according to a person's age, income, and education.*

- Once you have your preliminary introduction and thesis, get to work on your first draft of your paper. You can return to the first paragraph and revise it into an acceptable college introduction after you have completed the first draft. (*A word of warning:* Do *not* turn in a paper with a preliminary introduction. You must revise it into a more complete and polished piece of writing.)

Include a Thesis Statement as the Last Sentence of the Introduction

We've already made this point in the previous chapter, but it cannot be stressed enough. All good writing demands clarity, but college writing (as well as most business writing) requires that your main idea be up front and clear from the very start. Generally, that means the thesis should appear at the end

16

of your introduction. If you are writing a longer paper with an introduction consisting of several paragraphs, place the thesis at the end of the last introductory paragraph.

Types of Introductions

There are many ways to write successful introductions to college papers, but all involve introducing the topic and ending with a thesis statement. Here are some common introductory patterns.

❖ General to Specific

The general-to-specific introduction is the most common one in college writing. Its first few sentences introduce the topic in a general way and then move to the specific thesis statement of the paper. Here's an example:

GENERAL STATEMENTS TO MORE SPECIFIC STATEMENTS	*At one time or another, everyone has seen or read about the problem of the homeless persons in our society. Some people think homeless people are lazy and shiftless, unwilling to work for a living; others see them as victims of an unforgiving economic system; and still others see the homeless as emotionally or mentally defective, unable to function in society. Interestingly, everyone seems to have some kind of reaction to homeless people. There are not many neutral responses. And what is even more interesting is that most responses tell us quite a bit about the background of the person who*
THESIS STATEMENT	*is giving the response. Attitudes toward the homeless, in fact, vary significantly according to one's age, income, and education.*

❖ Opening Anecdote

Many successful papers open with a brief story or anecdote that directly relates to the thesis of the paper. An anecdote in your introduction can provide a sense of drama and immediacy that the general-to-specific opening might lack. However, if you use such an opening, you must be sure to include a clear statement of your topic and thesis before you end your introduction.

ANECDOTE	*Last weekend, my family and I were visiting Balboa Park when we passed one of the many homeless people who sleep in that park at night. His dirty hair was long and matted, and his clothes looked as if he hadn't*

washed them for over two months. When my father looked at him in disgust and muttered something about his being a worthless drain on society, my sister became quite angry. She said that he deserved sympathy, that he probably was a victim of circumstances beyond his control. Their differing reactions to that homeless man are not unusual. If anything, they tell us more about my sister and my father than about the homeless man him-

Thesis statement *self. In fact, attitudes toward the homeless vary significantly according to one's age, income, and education.*

❖ Opening Quotation

Quoting a sentence or two from a source related to your topic can be a very effective way to open an introduction. If you have done any research at all to develop your ideas, one of your sources may have a sentence that would provide a perfect opening to your essay.

Quotation *"Everybody hates the homeless. We pretend to feel sympathy for them, but really we all despise what they stand for." That, at least, is what Robert Parker says in his book* Independence: Something We Work For. *Although his opinion is rather extreme, it does raise the interesting question of how people do react to the homeless. Interestingly, everyone seems to have some kind of reaction to homeless people. There are not many neutral responses. And what is even more interesting is that most responses tell us quite a bit about a person's background.*

Thesis statement *Attitudes toward the homeless, in fact, vary significantly according to one's age, income, and education.*

What Not to Include in an Introduction

❖ Needless Dictionary Definitions

You should always define terms that an average reader may not be familiar with, but it's silly (as well as condescending) to quote a dictionary for terms the reader already knows. Don't start a paper like this: *According to* Webster's New Collegiate Dictionary, *a "home" is "a family's place of residence."* Everybody knows what a "home" is, so there is no need to quote from a dictionary.

❖ **Formal Announcements**

Instead of making statements about the topic, formal announcements make statements about the writer or about the paper itself. Avoid openings like these:

In my paper, I will discuss . . .
This paper will be about . . .
My first point will be . . .

OPENING EACH BODY PARAGRAPH WITH A TOPIC SENTENCE

As you write your paper, each paragraph after the introduction should present one point in support of or in explanation of your thesis statement. If you have organized your ideas already (see the chapter "Organizing Your Points"), you'll know what point each paragraph should focus on. Now you need to state that point in a clear topic sentence.

Write a Preliminary Topic Sentence

A preliminary topic sentence states the main idea of a particular paragraph. It is, essentially, the point that the paragraph will prove with facts, examples, explanations, and other types of support. Just as you did with the thesis statement, you should write a *preliminary* topic sentence, one that you will revise after you have completed the paragraph.

Place the Topic Sentence at the Start of the Paragraph

Clarity is important here. You want your reader to understand what your point is right away. Then you will proceed to prove or explain the point. So place the topic sentence at the start of the paragraph.

The Topic Sentence Should Support the Thesis Statement

Since your thesis statement expresses the main idea of your paper, each topic sentence should support that main idea. One way to make sure it does is to repeat words and phrases from the thesis. Note how the following topic sentences clearly echo the thought of the thesis statement while introducing the particular topic of each paragraph.

Thesis statement	*Although giving birth to a child is a wonderful thing, the **changes** that occur in the life of the new parents can often create **unexpected problems**.*
Topic sentence	*One **common change** is that the new parents' social life practically disappears, often resulting in **resentment** on the part of the husband or wife.*
Topic sentence	*A new child also brings with it increased financial responsibilities, and the resulting money concerns often cause **unexpected stress** between the new parents.*

Topic sentence: *One of the most **traumatic changes** is that the new parents have much less time alone.*

The Topic Sentence Should Not Merely State a Fact

A fact, by definition, does not need support or explanation, so statements of fact cannot be topic sentences. Note the difference between the following two statements:

Fact: *On August 12, 1996, a widespread power outage occurred in California, Oregon, Arizona, Nevada, and New Mexico.*

Topic Sentence: *The August 12, 1996, power outage, which affected California, Oregon, Arizona, Nevada, and New Mexico, was the result of two events that occurred almost simultaneously.*

As you can see, the fact requires no explanation, but the topic sentence does.

The Topic Sentence Should Not Be Too Vague, General, or Broad

Although the topic sentence should not state a specific fact, it also should not make too vague or general a statement. For instance, if your thesis is that a particular movie or play is a successful production and that it is worth seeing, your topic sentences would most likely introduce a number of reasons that the play or movie is successful. Those reasons should be as specific as you can make them in each topic sentence.

Vague topic sentence: *The character of Isabel was really interesting.*

Effective topic sentence: *The actress who portrayed Isabel was particularly good at conveying the pain and frustration of that character.*

Both topic sentences above are about the actress who played Isabel, but the first one could cover almost anything. The second one focuses only on how she conveys the pain and frustration of the character.

Developing Your Body Paragraphs with Supporting Sentences

Use Examples, Facts, and References to Authority

Supporting sentences consist of examples, facts, and references to authority to support the main idea expressed in the topic sentence.

- **Examples** can be drawn from your own experiences or from your reading, whichever is appropriate for the paper you are writing. In one paragraph you can use one long example or several brief examples. Generally, however, the more examples you can give, the more convincing your support will be.

- **Facts** are statements that have been shown to be true through direct observation, measurement, or experience. Statistics are facts. So are historical or current events and verified scientific observations.

- **References to authority** consist of statements and observations made by recognized experts in the field you are discussing. Usually you will get such material from outside reading or interviews. When you use expert opinion as support for controversial issues, remember that experts can disagree, so one expert's opinion may not be enough to prove your point.

If You Can, Blend the Three Types of Support

A paragraph that uses all three types of support—examples, facts, and references to authority—can be very convincing. There is no requirement that you use all three types in one paragraph, and many times it is impossible to do so, yet watch for opportunities to use all three.

Explain How the Support Relates to the Topic Sentence

As you provide examples, facts, and references to authority, don't assume that the reader will see how they support your topic sentence. Instead, *explain* how each point supports the main idea of the paragraph. Note, for example, how the support in the following paragraph is explained.

Topic sentence	*The actress who portrayed Isabel was particularly good at conveying the pain and frustration of that char-*
Supporting example	*acter. In the third act of the play, for example, when trying to decide whether or not to leave her husband,*

Explanation
of support

Isabel looked and sounded almost as if she were physically ill. Her forehead was creased, she staggered once or twice, and her voice kept starting to crack. Each of her actions clearly conveyed the mental and emotional agony she was experiencing. Her staggering walk was particularly effective. As she stumbled across the stage, the audience could almost feel her pain, frustration, and anger.

Use Specific Details

A specific detail gives actual names of places, people, and things. It provides dates, colors, sights, and sounds. It is descriptive, providing a picture for the reader. Notice the difference between the following two paragraphs.

General examples

During the summer, the beaches on the West Coast are crowded with people from all walks of life. For example, last year while I was on vacation at the beach, I met the vice president of a large corporation one day and a farm worker the next day. I even got to know a person who gave tours in the swamps in the South.

Examples with
specific details

During the summer, the beaches on the West Coast are crowded with people from all walks of life. For example, last August while I was on vacation at Laguna Beach, just north of San Juan Capistrano, I met the forty-year-old vice president of Coca-Cola Bottling Company. He was visiting from Atlanta, Georgia, and was enjoying lying on the beach all day without having to worry about the health of his company. The next day, while I was watching a baby octopus in a tidepool, I met a rough-looking young farmhand from Henderson, Kentucky. He said he was more used to seeing hundreds of acres of corn and soybeans than hundreds of miles of deep blue sea. Then, on the last day of my vacation, I met a woman who operated an airboat in the Everglades in Florida. She said that what she enjoyed most about the ocean was that she didn't have to worry about crocodiles lurking just below the surface.

How to Write Longer Paragraphs

If your paragraphs are too brief, you can develop them by:

- Adding more examples, facts, and references to authority
- Explaining each type of support more thoroughly
- Giving more specific details for each type of support

Don't try to write longer paragraphs by stretching out simple ideas with lots of extra words. Also, don't use larger margins or big type to try to fake a longer paper.

Writing a Concluding Paragraph

The Purpose of a Conclusion

A strong conclusion will not redeem a weak paper, but it can add a sense of completeness and clarity to even a mediocre one. Usually a successful concluding paragraph emphasizes the writer's intention, and often it provides some kind of reflection, question, or statement that the writer wants to leave with the reader.

Restate the Thesis Idea

In most conclusions, it is a good idea to emphasize the main point of your paper once again. But don't simply repeat the thesis statement from the introduction word-for-word. Instead, restate the *idea* of the thesis. Since you have now written the entire paper, you will probably find that you can express the idea of the paper more precisely and convincingly than you could when you wrote your preliminary thesis.

Types of Conclusions

Conclusions vary widely, depending on the content of the essay itself. The following list presents some elements found in many concluding paragraphs.

- A restatement of the thesis (but not a word-for-word repetition of the thesis statement)
- A summary of the supporting points presented in the body of your paper
- A prediction or recommendation
- A solution to a problem you have raised
- A quotation that supports the main idea of your paper
- A reference to an anecdote or example that appeared in your introduction or in the body of your paper

Here are some concluding paragraphs that use a few of the elements above.

Summary of supporting points

Given the overwhelming evidence that violent TV has deleterious effects on children, that it increases the level of violence throughout American society, it hardly seems unreasonable that the government ask that [the] TV industry tone down its violent programming. Those

Recommendation   *who find that request objectionable should forfeit their*
                      privileged use of public airwaves.
                      —Joseph Perkins, "It's a Prime-Time Crime"

Restatement   *But although you can never fully understand an-*
of thesis idea   *other's body language—or fully control your own—you*
                      can be aware that nonverbal cues are as important to
                      communication as words. Increase your knowledge of
                      body language, and you'll be a little less confused in a
Prediction   *world of many different messages.*
                      — Gerald Astor, "What Your Body Language Says
                      About You"

Reference to   *Thanks to that morning's conversion, I am a new*
anecdote from   *person. Now, I know I'll have to work hard. The sun*
essay   *streaming over the eastern Sierras wiped out the dark*
                      clouds that blurred my vision. Jonathan Harker in Bram
                      Stoker's "Dracula" must have felt exactly the same way
Quotation   *when he wrote in his journal: "No man knows 'till he*
                      has suffered from the night how sweet and how dear to
                      his heart and eye the morning can be."
                      —Joseph T. O'Connor, "A View from Mount Ritter"

What Not to Include in a Conclusion

- Don't restate your thesis or introduction word-for-word.

- Don't introduce a new subject or new idea that requires further support to be convincing.

- Don't draw conclusions that are not reasonably supported by your paper. For example, if you have been arguing that sexual preference is determined by genetic background, don't conclude by saying that upbringing never affects sexual preference. Proving that one's genetic background does affect sexuality does not prove that one's upbringing does not also affect it.

- Don't preach or threaten. Most people respond to suggestions more readily than to commands.

Revising the Paper

Do Not Confuse Revising with Editing

Revising consists of reworking your paper to improve the larger elements of composition: the thesis, organization, topic sentences, support, transitions, sentence variety, and word choice. Editing consists of correcting grammar, spelling, and punctuation errors.

Don't confuse the two. Correcting the grammar, spelling, and punctuation of your paper will not do much to improve it if it is poorly developed and unorganized. Revise first; then edit.

Refine Your Thesis

The thesis you started with was a *preliminary* one. It stated your central idea as best it could before the actual paper was written. Now that you have a complete draft, revise the thesis so it more accurately states the central idea of your paper. Look to the concluding paragraph. You may find there a clear statement of your thesis idea. If you do, use that statement as your thesis in the introduction and then rewrite the conclusion.

Check the Organization

Now that the first draft is written, you are in a better position to judge the placement of your paragraphs. If some paragraphs are clearly more important than others, consider putting them at the end so that your paper builds to them. If you are presenting comparisons or contrasts, organize the paragraphs so that they easily balance with each other. If you are following a chronological (time) progression, make sure that none of the points are presented out of the correct time sequence.

Clarify the Topic Sentences

Examine each paragraph to make sure it opens with an accurate topic sentence. In addition to stating the main idea of the paragraph, each topic sentence should clearly develop the central idea of the thesis statement. Try reading *only* the thesis statement and the topic sentences. You should be able to follow the train of thought in your paper when you do so.

Develop the Supporting Material

If your draft is too brief, you may need to add more paragraphs or more support within the existing paragraphs. Adding more paragraphs means developing new points to support your thesis, a problem that might require more research, freewriting, and brainstorming. Adding more support to your existing paragraphs involves developing more facts, examples, and references to authority to support the points that you already have. It also might mean explaining in more detail the support you already have.

Improve Your Transitions

- Transitions indicate a movement from one thought to another, or from a general statement to an example, or from an example to an explanation. They often are words and phrases such as *in addition, for example, therefore,* or *as a result.* Transitions also consist of repeated words or ideas as your paper moves from one sentence or paragraph to another. Here is a list of commonly used transitional words and phrases.

Time	*then, soon, first, second, finally, meanwhile, next, at first, in the beginning*
Contrast	*yet, but, however, instead, otherwise, on the other hand, on the contrary*
Addition	*and, also, besides, furthermore, in addition, likewise, moreover, similarly*
Cause-effect	*for, because, consequently, so, therefore, hence, thus, as a result*
Example	*for example, for instance, that is, such as*
Conclusion	*thus, hence, finally, generally, as a result, in conclusion*

- To improve your transitions, first look at the opening of each paragraph. Does it include a transition that moves it smoothly away from the point in the previous paragraph? For example, after a paragraph discussing jogging as a cardiovascular exercise, you might open a paragraph on weight training with this transition: <u>*In addition to jogging for the cardiovascular benefit,*</u> *one should consider weight training for the benefits it provides.*

- After you have examined the transitions at the start of each paragraph, look within the paragraphs. Add transitions to introduce new examples, facts, or other support as well as to move from support to explanation.

Vary the Length and Structure of Your Sentences

- If most of your sentences are about the same *length,* vary them by combining some to create longer sentences and dividing others to create shorter ones.

- Most sentences in college writing tend to follow the same *structure.* They start out with a main clause and then add whatever ideas are needed. These are called *cumulative* sentences. Here are two examples:

  main clause
  <u>*Our flight was late*</u> *because it was delayed by the snowstorm in Chicago.*

  main clause
  <u>*Ernest sat back in his chair and let out a loud sigh*</u> *after eating all of his meal.*

- Add some variety to your writing by changing some of your cumulative sentences into *periodic* ones. Periodic sentences open with a phrase or subordinate clause, putting the main clause off until the last part of the sentence.

  main clause
  Because it was delayed by the snowstorm in Chicago, <u>*our flight was late.*</u>

  main clause
  After eating all of his meal, <u>*Ernest sat back in his chair and let out a loud sigh.*</u>

(See the chapter "Varying Sentence Length and Structure" for more on sentence variety.)

Improve the Word Choice

Improve word choice by eliminating words that are unnecessary, repetitive, or redundant, by adding color to the details and examples you already have, and by adjusting the level of your vocabulary without sounding stilted, ornate, or "flowery." Most college papers should have a semi-formal tone to them. Avoid slang and overly informal words ("dude") and ones that are so formal that they make you sound pretentious ("prognosticate" for "predict"). See the chapters "Not Too Formal—Not Too Informal," "Avoiding Clichés and Euphemisms," and "Cutting Excess Words" for more thorough discussions of word choice.

EDITING AND PROOFREADING THE PAPER

EDITING

When you edit, you improve specific sentences and words as well as correct errors in grammar, spelling, and punctuation. Editing is an important step in the writing process. In most college classes, a paper that is poorly edited will not receive a passing grade even if the content is good.

Watch for Fragments and Run-On Sentences

You want to avoid all grammatical errors, but some are more serious than others. Fragments and run-on sentences tell the reader that you do not know even the basic rules of sentence writing. Before you print the final draft of your paper, read it carefully for these errors. Read the chapters "Recognizing Complete Sentences," "Sentence Fragments," and "Run-On Sentences" for help with these errors.

Check Your Verbs and Pronouns

Verbs and pronouns account for a great number of grammatical errors. Your verbs might switch tenses for no reason, or you might have used a plural verb with a singular subject. Pronoun case (*I* vs. *me; she* vs. *her*) causes problems for many students, as does pronoun number (*he or she* vs. *they; him or her* vs. *them*). If you have trouble in these areas, review the chapters "Subject-Verb Agreement," "Consistency in Verb Tense," "Pronoun Agreement," "Pronoun Reference," and "Pronoun Case."

Check the Spelling

If you use a computer, run a spell-check program. But don't rely too much on it. Spelling checkers will not point out errors such as confusing *there, their,* and *they're*. After you have run the spell-check program, read through the draft on your own. Look up the spelling of any words you are unsure of. The chapters "Commonly Confused Words" and "Spelling" will help you too.

Use Apostrophes Correctly

All punctuation is important, but many people today seem to be at a complete loss when it comes to apostrophe usage. Papers with misplaced or missing apostrophes have the same effect on an educated reader as someone smiling with a piece of spinach stuck between his front teeth. Read the chapter "Apostrophes" if you are confused about how to use apostrophes.

PROOFREADING

Proofreading is the final step, the last check before you decide that your paper is ready to be submitted to your instructor. To proofread successfully, you need to read your paper slowly and carefully, concentrating not on the ideas but on the words and letters themselves.

Proofread After You Print

If you are composing on a computer, you will naturally edit out any errors that you see on the screen. But do not assume that you have caught all of the errors once you have edited the screen. *Print a copy of your paper and proofread that printed copy.* You will be surprised at the number of errors you did not see on the screen.

Read from Back to Front

Reading from the last sentence to the first sentence helps you to focus on one sentence at a time without being distracted by the content of your paper. This technique is especially effective if you consistently repeat the same kind of error.

Ask Someone Else to Read Your Paper

Most colleges and universities provide free tutorial services. Usually you can bring a draft of your paper to the tutoring center and receive excellent feedback that will guide you not only in the proofreading but also in the writing, revising, and editing of your paper. If you can't use a tutor, even an acquaintance can often offer useful advice or point out errors you might have missed.

FORMATTING THE PAPER

Submitting a college paper is something like showing up for a job interview: Your knowledge and experience are what count, but how you look, speak, and present yourself can determine whether or not you are hired. Treat each college paper with the same care and respect you would use to dress for an interview.

Paper

- Use good quality white, 8½ × 11 paper.
- Don't use colored paper, thin paper, or odd-sized paper.
- Separate computer fan-fold paper and remove perforated edges.
- Paper clip or staple the pages together in the upper left corner.

Print

- Use black print.
- If your print is too light, replace your ink cartridge.
- If you have a choice of font and size, choose a standard font (Times Roman, Courier, Geneva, or Helvetica), usually in 12 point.
- Don't choose a style of print that draws attention to itself (such as a script style).
- Don't type in all capitals, italics, or boldface.

Margins and Justification

- Use one-inch margins all around the paper.
- Don't justify (align) the right margin of your paper. (Lining up the right side of a paper creates additional spacing between letters and words in a line, making your paper hard to read.)

Titles and Title Pages

- Capitalize only the first letter of each word in the title.
- Don't capitalize *a, an,* or *the,* prepositions, or coordinating conjunctions unless they are the first or last words of the title. (*Note:* The length of the word is not a factor. "Is" and "It" are capitalized, for example.)

- Do not underline or use quotation marks around the title of your paper.
- If your instructor requires a title page, center the title there. Place the following material below it in the lower half of the page.

    Your name
    The course title and number
    Your instructor's name
    The date

- If your instructor does not require a title page, place the above material in the upper left corner of the paper. Then double-space and type the title in the center of the next line. Double-space again and start typing your paper.

Typing

- Type on only one side of each page.
- Double-space between lines.
- Indent each paragraph five spaces (or use the "tab" key once).
- Do not skip extra lines between paragraphs.

Spacing and Punctuation Marks

- Don't space *before* a punctuation mark.
- Space one time after

    Periods
    Question marks
    Exclamation marks
    (However, if you are using a typewriter, not a word processor, space twice after these marks.)

- Space one time after

    Commas
    Semicolons
    Colons

- Never start a line with a punctuation mark. (If your word processor prints a line starting with a punctuation mark, you have accidentally typed a space before that mark. Delete the space.)
- For a dash, type two hyphens (--) with no space before, after, or between them.
- For an ellipsis, type three periods (. . .) with a space before and after each period.

Dividing Words

- Don't divide words unless you have to. Most word processors will move a word that is too long down to the next line, and that is better than dividing a word unnecessarily.

- Divide words at syllable breaks. If you don't know where a syllable ends, use a dictionary. Dots will appear between the syllables.

- Never divide a one-syllable word.

- Never divide a word after only one letter.

Correcting Errors

- If you are using a typewriter, proofread your page before you take it out of the typewriter. You can correct minor errors using lift-off tape or white-out. Major errors will require that you retype the page.

- If you are using a word processor, proofread your page both before *and after* you print a copy of it. Make any corrections and then reprint your paper.

- Typographical errors are still errors. If you find one at the last minute, when it is too late to print a new copy, some instructors will accept one or two *neat* corrections in black ink (*not* blue ink or pencil). Check with your teacher.

Composing on a Computer

Computers are marvelous tools that have transformed the process of writing for many people. If you compose on a computer, you already know the many advantages of being able to move text easily and quickly, save multiple versions of the same work, and revise and re-revise with a few keystrokes.

However, regardless of your experience, there are a few points all writers should remember when composing on a computer.

Save Your Work as You Go Along

Save your work at least every fifteen minutes. If your program has an automatic save feature, turn it on. There is nothing worse than losing your entire paper when your computer freezes simply because you have not taken a few seconds to save a document.

Always Make a Backup Copy of Your Work on a Separate Disk

If you are working on your school's computer, buy a separate disk and carry it with you so that you can back up your work. School computers can crash just as those at home can. If you have a backup copy, your work won't be lost if (or when) that computer crashes.

Always Use the Spelling Checker

But don't rely on the spelling checker alone. It won't recognize the difference between *there* and *their* or *through* and *threw*. After you have used the spelling checker, read the draft yourself and correct the spelling errors that the checker missed.

Always Proofread a *Printed* Copy of Your Work

Do not merely proofread the copy on the screen of your computer. You will find many errors and weaknesses on the printed copy that you did not see on the screen itself.

Be Wary of Programs that Check Grammar and Style

Although some grammar and style checkers offer helpful suggestions, most are quite cumbersome and confusing. The problem all such programs face is that grammar and style are dependent on the meaning and context of your sentences. As a result, your grammar and style cannot be "checked" in the objective way that your spelling can.

PART 2

SPECIAL ASSIGNMENTS

THE IN-CLASS PAPER AND ESSAY EXAMINATION

READING ACTIVELY AND ACCURATELY

WRITING A SUMMARY

THE RESEARCH PAPER

DOCUMENTING YOUR SOURCES

SAMPLE RESEARCH PAPER

The In-Class Paper and Essay Examination

Not many college activities cause more stress and anxiety than in-class papers and essay exams. However, both types of writing are an inescapable part of college life, but there are a number of steps you can take to improve your performance in these areas.

Preparing for the Essay Exam

- To write a successful essay exam, you must know the material that the exam will cover. Make an outline of the major and minor points from your text as well as from your class notes. Try to summarize those points into key words and phrases. Memorizing those words and phrases will help you to remember the points you need to know.

- Anticipate the exam questions. You have been listening to your instructor all semester long, so you know what *might* appear on the exam. Prepare answers to several possible questions. For instance, if you are studying for an exam in American history and you have been discussing the major battles of the Civil War in class, you might anticipate an essay question like "Give three major reasons that the North won the Battle of Gettysburg."

Preparing for the In-Class Paper

- If you are given the topic in advance or if you are given several topics, one of which you will be asked to write on, prepare for the in-class essay by writing out a complete paper at home on each of the topics. Doing so will help you organize your points and develop specific examples for each one. And writing out the full paper will help you figure out how to word your sentences to express your points clearly. Of course, you can't bring that paper to class, but you will write a much more effective in-class essay with this kind of preparation.

- If you are not given the topic in advance, there is not much you can do to prepare for it. Just make sure that you know the basic elements of any essay: introduction, thesis statement, body paragraphs, topic sentences, specific support, and conclusion.

Getting Started

- Once you are in class and are given the question(s) or assignment, the process is similar for both types. You still need to do some planning and preparing before beginning your essay.

- Before you begin, read very carefully the question you must respond to. Underline the words that tell you what you must do in your essay. If the question asks you to discuss the *causes* of an event, a mere *description* of the event is not enough. If it asks you to discuss *causes and effects*, an analysis of just the causes will not be enough. Other essay questions might ask you to *identify several characteristics* of a topic. Or they might ask you to explain the *similarities or differences* between two topics. Whatever the question is, underline the key terms and prepare answers that respond to those terms.

- After carefully reading the question, you will be tempted to start writing the essay at once (after all, time is passing), but don't give in to that temptation. Instead, take five minutes to do some fast brainstorming. Let's say you have been asked to write a personal essay explaining how three events have influenced your life. Make a list of important events, like your first date, your first car, the death of your father, your trip to Vancouver, your first speech on the debate team, or your promotion to shift supervisor. Then choose the three most important ones: your father's death, your participation on the debate team, and your promotion to shift supervisor.

- Now you can write your thesis statement and make a plan. Your thesis statement can be as simple as "The three events that have had the most powerful effect on my life so far are the death of my father, the first speech I ever gave on the debate team, and my promotion to shift supervisor." The plan of your essay might look like this:

  1. *Two sentences about events and background, leading to thesis statement*

  2. *First body paragraph about death of my father when I was ten*

  3. *Second body paragraph about my first speech on the debate team and the sense of accomplishment and confidence it gave me*

  4. *Third body paragraph about promotion to shift supervisor and gaining of sense of responsibility and sense of achievement*

  5. *Concluding sentences about the overall effects of these experiences*

Writing the Paper

As you begin your paper, keep these ideas in mind.

- Stick to your plan. Don't change your mind in the middle of your essay.
- Be specific. Give plenty of concrete examples to support your ideas. For example, it is not enough to say that your first speech on the debate team gave you confidence. Describe how you felt as you approached the podium, what you saw as you looked into the audience, what you thought as you saw the interest in the judges' eyes, how you felt as you wrapped up. Tell the reader what that speech taught you about yourself and your abilities.
- Don't pad your paper with needless extra words. Although adding specific details and examples will improve a paper, using twenty words to write what should be written in ten will weaken it. Let your specific examples carry the day.
- Bring and use your dictionary, thesaurus, or electronic spelling checker as allowed by your instructor. Spelling will count.
- Don't plan on having time to revise your paper. Instead, write your first draft as neatly and as carefully as possible. Write on only one side of each page and skip lines if your instructor asks you to.
- If you need to add material after you have already written the paper, write an asterisk (*) or a number (1, 2, 3 . . .) where the material should be inserted. Then write the new material (preceded by an asterisk or number) either at the bottom of the page or at the end of the paper.
- If you need to delete something, draw a neat single line through it. Don't obliterate it with a messy scrawl of ink.
- Use any time you have left to proofread carefully, making neat pen-and-ink corrections as necessary.

READING ACTIVELY AND ACCURATELY

In many—perhaps most—of your college papers, you will need to use or respond to reading material that might come from your textbook, from class handouts, from library research, or from any number of other sources. To use reading material effectively, you need to do more than just read well: You need to read actively and accurately.

Establish Your Expectations

- *Before* you read, take a moment to think. Consider the title of the chapter, article, or book. Does it raise any questions in your mind? Does it suggest a topic or point that you should look for as you read? Consider any background information that accompanies the reading selection. What does it suggest about the author or the reading material?

- Thinking about these questions should take only a minute or two, but these few minutes are important. They will help you to understand more of what you read because you are starting your reading with a focused, active attitude.

First Reading: Underline or Highlight as You Read

- With a pen, pencil, or highlighter in hand, read the material from start to finish, slowly and carefully. During the first reading, you're trying to get an overall sense of the main idea of the selection. Don't try to take notes yet. Instead, just underline or highlight whatever sentences seem important to you. If a sentence seems to state a significant idea, mark it. If an example or fact is particularly striking, mark it too. If you come across words that you do not recognize, circle or mark them.

Second Reading: Annotate

- *Don't skip this step.* This activity separates the mediocre from the above-average reader. Here you really begin to *comprehend* what you have just read.

- Re-read the sentences you have marked. As you do, use a pen or pencil to write brief notes in the margins to identify the ideas in those sentences. You won't need to write a note for every marked sentence. As you read the places you have underlined or highlighted, you will realize that some of them are not very important after all. So skip them.

- Completing this step will help you comprehend what you have read as you begin to recognize both the main idea of the reading selection and the organization of its supporting material.

Outline the Main and Supporting Ideas

- Whether you outline the entire reading selection depends upon how well you need to understand it. If you are studying for a test on the reading material, a complete outline is essential. However, if you are using only portions of the selection, as is common in a research paper, you need to outline only those particular ideas that you will use in your paper.

- In either case, you should first write out the main idea of the entire selection *in your own words*. Try to express that idea in only one or two sentences. Below that main idea, write out each supporting idea as clearly and accurately as you can. You must be very careful here. Don't distort or change the author's ideas as you outline them.

Respond to the Reading Material

- Your reaction to what you have read is important, especially if your instructor will expect you to evaluate or respond to the reading material in a test or if you intend to use it in a research paper. Do you find the points you have noted convincing? Does your own experience, or other material you have read, confirm or contradict it? Write down your own responses now, before you have moved on to other reading material.

Sample Annotated Reading Selection

topic

THE DECLINE OF NEATNESS
Norman Cousins

the "sloppiness virus"

thesis

blue jeans as a symbol

Anyone with a passion for hanging labels on people or things should have little difficulty in recognizing that an apt tag for our times is the Unkempt Generation. I am not referring solely to college kids. The sloppiness virus has spread to all sectors of society. People go to all sorts of trouble and expense to look uncombed, unshaved, unpressed.

The symbol of the times is blue jeans—not just blue jeans in good condition but jeans that are frayed, torn, discolored. They don't get that way naturally. No one wants blue jeans that are crisply clean or spanking new. Manufacturers recognize a big market when they see it, and they compete with one another to offer jeans that are made to look as though they've just been discarded by clumsy house painters after ten years of wear. The more faded and seemingly ancient the garment, the higher the cost. Disheveled is in fashion; neatness is obsolete.

clothing—a slavish conformity

Nothing is wrong with comfortable clothing. It's just that current usage is more reflective of a slavish conformity than a desire for ease. No generation has strained harder than ours to affect a casual, relaxed, cool look; none has succeeded more spectacularly in looking as though it had been stamped out by cookie cutters. The attempt to avoid any appearance of being well groomed or even neat has a quality of desperation about it and suggests a calculated and phony deprivation. We shun conventionality, but we put on a uniform to do it. An appearance of alienation is the triumphant goal, to be pursued in oversize sweaters and muddy sneakers.

slovenly speech

Slovenly speech comes off the same spool. Vocabulary, like blue jeans, is being drained of color and distinction. A complete sentence in everyday speech is as rare as a man's tie in the swank Polo Lounge of the Beverly Hills Hotel. People communicate in chopped-up phrases, relying on grunts and chants of "you know" or "I mean" to cover up a damnable incoherence. Neat-

neatness is needed in language too

ness should be no less important in language than it is in dress. But spew and sprawl are taking over. The English language is one of the greatest sources of wealth in the world. In the midst of accessible riches, we are linguistic paupers.

violence in language

Violence in language has become almost as casual as the possession of handguns. The curious notion has taken hold that emphasis in communicating is impossible without the incessant use of four-letter words. Some screenwriters openly admit that they

screenwriters and foul language

are careful not to turn in scripts that are devoid of foul language lest the classification office impose the curse of a G (general) rating. Motion-picture exhibitors have a strong preference for the R (restricted) rating, probably on the theory of forbidden fruit. Hence writers and producers have every incentive to employ tasteless language and gory scenes.

attitudes of casualness toward violence and brutality

The effect is to foster attitudes of casualness toward violence and brutality not just in entertainment but in everyday life. People are not as uncomfortable as they ought to be about the glamorization of human hurt. The ability to react instinctively to suffering seems to be atrophying. Youngsters sit transfixed in front of television or motion-picture screens, munching popcorn while human beings are battered or mutilated. Nothing is more essential in education than respect for the frailty of human be-

mindless violence

ings; nothing is more characteristic of the age than mindless violence.

children will not outgrow these attitudes

desensitization

Everything I have learned about the educational process convinces me that the notion that children can outgrow casual attitudes toward brutality is wrong. Count on it: if you saturate young minds with materials showing that human beings are fit subjects for debasement or dismembering, the result will be desensitization to everything that should produce revulsion or resistance. The first aim of education is to develop respect for life, just as the highest expression of civilization is the supreme tenderness that people are strong enough to feel and manifest toward one another. If society is breaking down, as it too often appears to be, it is not because we lack the brain power to meet its demands but because our feelings are so dulled that we don't recognize we have a problem.

human relationships

casual sex deadens feelings

Untidiness in dress, speech, and emotions is readily connected to human relationships. The problem with the casual sex so fashionable in films is not that it arouses lust but that it deadens feelings and annihilates privacy. The danger is not that sexual exploitation will create sex fiends but that it may spawn eunuchs. People who have the habit of seeing everything and doing anything run the risk of feeling nothing.

maybe the sloppiness virus will run its course

My purpose here is not to make a case for a Victorian decorum or for namby-pambyism. The argument is directed to bad dress, bad manners, bad speech, bad human relationships. The hope has to be that calculated sloppiness will run its course. Who knows, perhaps some of the hip designers may discover they can make a fortune by creating fashions that are unfrayed and that grace the human form. Similarly, motion-picture and television producers and exhibitors may realize that a substantial audience exists for something more appealing to the human eye and spirit than the sight of a human being hurled through a store-front window or tossed off a penthouse terrace. There might even be a salutary response to films that dare to show people expressing genuine love and respect for one another in more convincing ways than anonymous clutching and thrashing about.

schools should encourage genuine creativity

Finally, our schools might encourage the notion that few things are more rewarding than genuine creativity, whether in the clothes we wear, the way we communicate, the nurturing of human relationships, or how we locate the best in ourselves and put it to work.

WRITING A SUMMARY

Clear and accurate summarizing is an important skill in many college classes. Your ability to summarize effectively will help you to study for and take tests, to write reports and papers, and to give thorough, convincing oral presentations. Summarizing, especially in research papers, requires documentation. See the chapter "Documenting Your Sources" for a discussion of this topic.

Characteristics of a Successful Summary

- It accurately communicates the author's central idea.
- It includes all of the author's supporting ideas.
- It usually does not include supporting facts, examples, and elaborations.
- It does not include your opinions or reactions.
- It does not alter the author's meaning in any way.
- It uses your own words and writing style.

Preparing to Write the Summary

- First Reading

  Read the material *actively,* as explained in the chapter "Reading Actively and Accurately." Underline or highlight whatever seems significant to you. Mark statements that seem to express the central and supporting ideas of the reading selection.

- Second Reading

  Re-read the material, annotating and dividing it into major sections so that each section reflects one supporting idea.

Writing the Summary

- Opening Sentence

  The opening sentence of your summary should identify the name of the reading selection, the author, and the central idea, purpose, thesis, or topic of the selection.

- Supporting Sentences

  After the opening sentence, briefly summarize each of the author's supporting ideas. Shorter reading selections will often require no more than one sentence to summarize each supporting idea.

Using Your Own Words and Writing Style

Although summaries may include a few brief direct quotations, for the most part you should use your own words. Consider these points:

- Use *your* writing style, not the author's. Do not simply change a few of the author's words in a sentence. Rewrite the entire idea.
- Use transitions that refer to the author as you move from one supporting point to the next.
- Use the present tense when referring to the author.

A Sample Summary

The following paragraph is a summary of Norman Cousins' "The Decline of Neatness," which you will find on pages 43–45.

> In "The Decline of Neatness," Norman Cousins argues that a "sloppiness virus" is affecting all areas of our society. According to Cousins, the sloppy clothing that is so fashionable today reflects our desperate need to conform, making us look as if we were "stamped out by cookie cutters." Our sloppy speech reflects the same need, but it goes beyond the slovenly to the violent. And this sloppily violent speech results in casual attitudes towards all violence and brutality. Cousins claims that we seem to be losing the ability to react to suffering. He says that the violence and brutality in movies and television are "desensitizing" our children and that such casual attitudes toward violence will not be outgrown. Finally, he suggests that our sloppy clothing, speech, and emotions affect human relationships, as is evident in the casual attitude toward sex in films, an attitude that is deadening our feelings and destroying our privacy. Cousins concludes by stating that he does not want to return to Victorian attitudes, although he does hope that our "calculated sloppiness" will soon disappear and that we will all begin to "locate the best in ourselves and put it to work."

THE RESEARCH PAPER

Writing a research paper may seem like an overwhelming task at first. But it really is not. Although research papers do take more time than shorter, less complicated essays, they certainly should not cause the worry and anxiety that so many students seem to feel when they think about research assignments. After all, a research paper is just an extended essay supported with material that you have found in outside sources.

GETTING STARTED

Choosing an Appropriate Topic

- Before you choose your topic, make sure you understand the assignment. If you are supposed to argue a point, your topic should be one that can be argued, such as whether or not gambling should be legalized in your state. If you are supposed to write a report rather than an argument, your topic should require explanation, not argument, such as an analysis of the effects of gambling on different personality types.

- Don't choose a topic that is too broad. If you have never written a research paper before, you might think that you need an extra large topic, but you don't. Trying to tackle a broad topic like the problems that gambling has caused different cultures throughout history will only result in a paper that covers many different points in a very superficial way. The length of a good research paper comes from fewer points discussed in depth, with many supporting ideas and facts drawn from research.

Developing a Thesis

- The thesis states the central idea of your paper. Usually it is written as the last sentence of the introduction. If you are writing an argument, it is the statement that your entire paper must prove. (*The drawbacks of legalized gambling in California far outweigh any benefits.*) If you are writing a factual report, it states the central point of the report. (*One of the basic causes of homelessness is mental illness, either clinical depression or schizophrenia.*)

- If you know what position you want to argue or what point you want to make, write a preliminary thesis statement and move on to your research. However, if you do not know where you stand on an issue, write a question that you want your research to answer. (*Should gambling be legalized in California? What are the primary causes of homelessness?*) Once you have completed your research, replace your question with a statement of the conclusion you have drawn. That conclusion will now serve as your thesis. Place it in the introduction.

DOING THE RESEARCH

Researching the Topic

First, some warnings about research: A research paper is not a paraphrase of an encyclopedia article, nor is it a patchwork of quotations from your sources. It is a presentation of *your ideas,* supported by research. In other words, *you* and *your ideas* are a major part of the paper, even if your ideas were not clearly formed before you began your research. That said, let's look at some of the best sources for your research.

Using Encyclopedias and Other Reference Books

Sometimes the best way to start your research is to read some general articles on your topic in encyclopedias or specialized reference works. You'll find these books in the reference section of the library. Use *The New Encyclopedia Britannica* or *Encyclopedia Americana.* Both will give you general articles written by experts on the subject and will provide lists of other works you should read. Ask your librarian what other specialized reference works will have material on your topic.

Using Books

Books are a primary research source, but they do have some drawbacks. In most cases, the books in a library are several years old, so some of the information in them can be outdated. Also, many books might contain valuable information on your topic in only one of their chapters, so plan to do some hunting through the table of contents of books that are on your general topic but not necessarily on the particular point you want to make.

Computerized Catalog Systems for Books

- Most libraries now have their books cataloged by computer, and most of the systems are relatively user-friendly and easy enough to figure out. Your best bet will be to enter a subject heading related to your topic (such as *gambling*). The computer will then provide you with a list of books discussing that subject. If the list is too long, you might try re-entering a more specific combination of words (usually using *and*), such as *legalized* and *gambling*.

- If you cannot figure out how to use the computer, talk to one of the librarians. They *enjoy* helping people search for material. That's why they became librarians in the first place. Before you look for the book itself, be sure to record its entire *call number* (a series of letters and numbers, usually toward the top or bottom of each entry on the computer) as well as the title and author's name.

Using Articles

Articles appear in periodicals (magazines, newspapers, and journals) and usually have the most current material on a topic. The quickest way to find out which periodicals contain articles on your topic is to use your library's computerized database.

Computerized Databases for Articles

- In most libraries, you will find a computerized listing of articles either on the same computers that list books or on a separate set of computers in the reference section. For the most part, use the computers for periodicals the same way you use the ones for books: Enter a subject heading or a combination of words and see what comes up. If you see titles that look promising, record the author, title of article, title of periodical, date, and page number of the source. (Often, you can print out this information rather than write it all down.) Also, check to see if your library's database includes the article itself. If you are lucky, you will be able to preview, read, and print the entire article without leaving the computer.

- *Before* you leave the computer, check to see if your library carries the periodical you need. Somewhere near you, perhaps on the computer itself, will be a list or a pamphlet identifying what periodicals your library carries and where they are located. If you don't see one, ask the librarian. Some periodicals will be collected as single magazines on shelves, others will be in bound volumes (one for each year), and still others will be on microfilm.

Older Articles

- Periodicals more than five years old are not usually indexed on computers. To find them, you will need to look in bound volumes (large books) that list articles by subject matter. These volumes are usually found on tables near the reference desk. Look for *The Readers' Guide to Periodical Literature.* It lists articles found in over one hundred general magazines. For more specialized topics, look at the *Education Index, Art Index, Business Periodical Index, Social Sciences Index,* or any of the other indexes related to the general area of your topic.

- *A word of advice:* Don't be discouraged by the technology or by the confusion that comes with your first attempt at periodical research. Ask for help. Tell the librarian you haven't done research before. After the first time, it becomes much easier.

Using the Internet

Be very careful with this source. Many libraries now provide Internet access, and more and more people have direct access at home. As you probably know, you can find a mountain of material on the Internet, using the same search techniques mentioned above. But you want reliable material from reputable sources, not the uneducated opinion of anyone at all. If you have any doubt about the reliability of an Internet source, ask your instructor before you use it.

Other Sources

You don't need to restrict your research to books and articles. Consider these sources also:

- **Videos, recordings, and multimedia material.** This material is usually found in a special media section of the library.
- **Pamphlet file** (sometimes called the vertical file, usually located near the reference desk). This file is a collection of pamphlets and clippings on a variety of topics. It is especially good for local items.
- **Interviews.** Sometimes you can interview professors, business leaders, community members, or experts in the area of your topic.

TAKING NOTES

- Before you take notes from any source at all, be sure to write down the information that you will need later for your Works Cited page:

For a book: *author, title, edition (if not the first), place of publication, publisher, and date of publication*

For an article: *author, title of article, title of publication, date, page numbers, volume and issue numbers*

For a computer database or the Internet: *same material as above, but also the name of the data base, date of electronic publication, date you visited the site, and Internet address*

- Make a copy of the article or portion of the book you intend to use. (Be sure to write all of the above publication information on the copy.) Now you can mark up this copy all you want.

- Read the source, underlining and highlighting major ideas and any places that seem to express significant points. Don't take notes yet. Just read and underline.

- Now take notes from what you have underlined. Use a separate sheet of paper (or note cards, if you prefer). As much as possible, use your own words in your notes. Next to each notation, identify the page number. If you write down *anything* word for word, place quotation marks around it and identify the page number.

- *A warning:* Some students skip taking notes and try to write their paper directly from the underlined material that they've read. Don't do it. The result is almost always a paper that reads like a string of loosely related quotations and summaries.

- When you have taken all of your notes, re-read them. Mark those that seem particularly important. As best you can, identify notes that discuss similar ideas even though they come from different sources.

Writing the Paper

Organizing Your Thoughts and Writing the First Draft

- Once you have completed your research, set it aside for a moment and spend some time writing out your own thoughts. After all, your paper should present your views, as informed by the research you have done. What seem to be the most important issues in what you have read? Have your own ideas changed at all? Check the thesis you started with. Does it still express the central idea that your research will support? If you should revise it, do so now.

- The best way to organize your material is to think through your paper from first paragraph to last, *writing a rough outline as you do*. **Don't skip this step.** The temptation now will be to start writing the essay itself. But you will find it *much easier* to write if you first think the paper through, writing down in brief phrases and sentences the basic ideas that you will include in each section of your paper. Write down your responses to questions like these:

Introduction	*What material should I include in my introduction?*
First section	*What point should the first section of the body of my paper discuss?*
	What material from my research should I include in this section? (Look through your notations from research to find material that should be included in your first section.)
	How many paragraphs will this section include?
Second and later sections	*Ask the same questions for each section and write brief notes in the form of a rough outline.*

- If you have prepared a thorough rough outline, you will now find it much easier to write the first full draft of the paper. Don't worry about the perfect writing style. Just follow your rough outline and present your ideas as clearly as you can.

Integrating Your Sources into Your Paper

- As you write your paper, you will present your ideas from research three ways: as direct quotations, paraphrases, and summaries.

Direct quotations	Direct quotations are word-for-word repetitions of the original source. Always place quotation marks around them. (Exception: Long quotations set off from the text do not use quotation marks.) Use direct quotations sparingly to avoid the appearance of a paper that is merely a string of quotations. No more than 10 to 15 percent of your paper should be direct quotation.
Paraphrases	Paraphrases are ideas from the original source written in your own words and writing style. Usually paraphrases are about the same length as the ideas were in their original form.
Summaries	Summaries are ideas from the original source written in your own words and writing style. They differ from paraphrases in that summaries usually condense several paragraphs or more from the original source into a few sentences.

- Each direct quotation, paraphrase, or summary should be *integrated* into your paper with a transition. Do not simply "dump" one into your paragraph. Compare the following examples:

"Dumped" quotation
: *Many people believe that the residents of homeless shelters are just lazy and unmotivated, but such a view is much too simplistic.* "Most people who end up in homeless shelters are suffering from schizophrenia, clinical depression, or post traumatic stress syndrome."

Quotation with transition
: *Many people believe that the residents of homeless shelters are just lazy and unmotivated, but such a view is much too simplistic.* According to a recent study by Daniel Moriarty, a Stanford psychologist, *"Most people who end up in homeless shelters are suffering from schizophrenia, clinical depression, or post traumatic stress syndrome."*

"Dumped" paraphrase
: *Many people believe that the residents of homeless shelters are just lazy and unmotivated, but such a view is much too simplistic. Many of them are suffering from serious mental and emotional disorders.*

Paraphrase with transition
: *Many people believe that the residents of homeless shelters are just lazy and unmotivated, but such a view is much too simplistic.* According to a recent study by Daniel Moriarty, a Stanford psychologist, *many of them are suffering from serious mental and emotional disorders.*

Avoiding Plagiarism

- Plagiarism occurs when you present someone else's words or ideas as if they were your own. When you directly quote from another work, you *must* use quotation marks as well as identify the source of the quotation. When you paraphrase or summarize from another work, you also *must* identify the source. Not doing so is plagiarism.

- A more subtle type of plagiarism occurs when you change only a few words in a passage, keeping most of the style of the original, and then present the passage as a paraphrase. When you paraphrase or summarize, use your own writing style. Try not to copy the style of the original. (See the chapter "Writing a Summary.")

DOCUMENTING YOUR SOURCES

If you use someone else's ideas, facts, examples, or statistics, you must *document* your source in two places:

- In *parenthetical references* within the body of the paper
- On the *Works Cited* page at the end of your paper

You must document sources even if you do not quote them directly, even if you only paraphrase or summarize the ideas of someone else. However, you do not need to document facts that are common knowledge (Neil Armstrong was the first person to walk on the moon).

PARENTHETICAL REFERENCES WITHIN THE BODY OF THE PAPER

Today's writers no longer use an elaborate footnote system together with Latin expressions at the bottom of the page. Instead, they use the method of the Modern Language Association (MLA) or the American Psychological Association (APA). Both methods use *parenthetical references,* although in slightly different ways. The following information is based on the MLA, the method used in English classes and the humanities.

Parenthetical References

Parenthetical references are placed within the paper directly after *all direct quotations, summaries, or paraphrases.* In them, you give readers just enough information so that they can find the full source on the Works Cited page at the end of your paper. The three most common parenthetical references are:

- Page number only   (187)
- Author and page number   (Royster 187)
- Title (or portion of title) and page number   ("Sherman's" 77)

Notice that no comma or *p* (for page) is used before the page numbers.

Page Number Only

This is the most common parenthetical reference. Use only a page number if you have already identified the author:

*According to Royster, "Both groups could see the defeat of the
Confederacy coming" (187).*

Since you have given the last name of the author within the sentence, the
reader can easily find the full source on your Works Cited page. The page
number is all that you need in parentheses.

Author and Page Number

Include the last name of the author in the parentheses if you have not yet
identified the author:

*Toward the spring of that year, the leaders of both armies knew that the
days of the Confederacy were numbered (Royster 187).*

Title and Page Number

Use the title within the parentheses if your source does not have an author
listed and if you haven't already mentioned the title in your text. You do not
need to use the entire title. Include just enough of it to lead the reader to the
right place on your Works Cited page.

*The bitterness has become "rancid in the veins of Southerners"
("Sherman's" 77).*

The entire title is "Sherman's March and Southern Attitudes," but one word
is all that is needed to lead the reader to the article on the Works Cited page.

Punctuation with Parenthetical References

Place the period that ends your sentence at the end of and outside the parentheses. Look at the examples above. Note that the period is placed after the
parentheses, not before them.

One exception: If you set off a quotation because it is more than four
typed lines long, the period is placed at the end of the last word, before the
parentheses.

Special Situations

❖ Secondhand Quotations

If your source quotes some *other* source, and you also want to quote that
other source, use "qtd. in" (quoted in):

❖ **Article in a Scholarly Journal**

Author. "Title of Article." <u>Title of Journal</u>. Volume Number (Date): Page number(s) of entire article.

Tolson, David. "Sherman's Dastardly Deed." <u>Annals of the Confederacy</u>. 55 (Dec. 1994): 367–80.

❖ **Encyclopedia**

Author (if there is one). "Title of Selection." <u>Title of Encyclopedia</u>. Date of the edition.

Jones, William K. "Sherman Anti-Trust Act." <u>Encyclopedia Americana</u>. 1989 ed.

Special Situations

❖ **No Author Given**

Use the first main word of the title. Alphabetize according to that word.

"The South's Anger." <u>The Knoxville Sentinel</u>. 25 Jan. 1945, Sec. E: 2–3.

❖ **More Than One Author**

Use the last name for first author only. List subsequent authors by first and last names.

Erianger, Steven and Alison Mitchell. "U.S. Officials Rethink Need To Deploy Troops." <u>The San Diego Union-Tribune</u>. 16 Nov. 1996, Sec. A: 1,19.

❖ **More Than One Work by the Same Author**

For entries after the first one, use three hyphens and a period in place of the author's name. Alphabetize the works by the titles.

Cornwell, Patricia. <u>The Body Farm</u>. New York: Scribner, 1994.

---. <u>From Potter's Field</u>. New York: Scribner, 1995.

❖ **Internet**

Author (if available). <u>Title</u>. [Title and dates of original source as listed above for magazines and newspapers.] <u>Name of source of electronic text or of Internet site</u>. Identifying number, if available. Date of access. <Electronic address.>

Arnsan, Dan. "The Alamo: A Scale Model and a Model for Teaching Research Skills." <u>Home page</u>. 1997. 20 Oct. 1998 <http:www.flash.net/,alamo3/documents/arnsan/arnsan.htm>.

❖ **Pamphlet**

Use the same format as for a book. Often the author will be an organization, like the Department of Defense.

❖ **Radio or Television Program**

<u>Name of Program</u>. Network. Local station, Broadcasting City. Date.
<u>A Prairie Home Companion</u>. NPR. St. Paul, Minnesota. 17 Nov. 1996.

❖ **Video or Audio Recording**

Author or director. <u>Title</u>. Format. Producer, Release date. Running time.
Hirsch, Henry. <u>The Civil War and the Twentieth Century</u>. CD. Warner
    Thompson, 1991. 120 min. (approx.).

❖ **Interview**

Name of person. Personal or phone. Date.
Shugs, Percy. Phone Interview. 16 Nov. 1996.

SAMPLE RESEARCH PAPER

Writer's name	Alan Buyayo
Instructor	Professor McDonald
Course	English 100
Date	16 May 1999

Title centered

Gun Control: A Need in America

Double-spaced throughout

The Second Amendment to the Constitution of the United States reads as follows: "A well regulated Militia, being necessary for the security of a free State, the right of the people to keep and bear Arms, shall not be infringed." To many people, these words are crystal clear. They guarantee the citizens of this country the right "to keep and bear Arms," and they guarantee that the right to do so "shall not be infringed." To other people, however, they are not so clear. Do they apply to all people at all times or just to the "Militia"? Do they prohibit any and all control of firearms? As with most controversial issues, what seems to be so obvious to so many people is really not very obvious at all. What is certain, however, is that many

Parenthetical reference includes part of title when author is not known

people oppose gun control. They feel that owning a gun makes a house a safer place ("Poll Shows" 46). In fact, so many people own guns in the United States that we can be said to have developed a "gun culture" in which owning a gun is normal behavior "across vast swaths of the social landscape"

Parenthetical reference includes last name of author if author not already identified in transition

(Wright 64). Such widespread gun ownership, however, does not negate the need for reasonable gun control, nor did the writers of the Second Amendment intend that guns never be regulated. There are, in fact, many valid reasons to carefully

Thesis statement

control the use of firearms in our country.

Topic sentence developing the thesis statement

One very simple reason for controlling gun ownership is that so many Americans support the idea. Survey after survey concludes that citizens of the United States want some kind of

61

Transition identifying author and article

gun control. Robert J. Blendon, in his article "The American Public and the Gun Control Debate," which appeared in the Journal of the American Medical Association, writes, "Both gun owners and nonowners express support for many specific gun control policies, including the recent Brady Act and the ban on semiautomatic assault weapons" (1723). Based on a study of fourteen opinion surveys conducted between 1956 and 1996, Blendon goes on to say that most Americans agree that minors as well as people with a history of criminal activity should be prohibited from owning guns (1723). In addition, an article in the American Medical News reports that a majority of people who do not own guns support the total banning of handguns altogether from the civilian population ("Poll Shows" 46). According to the same article, even gun owners often support some kind of gun control. For instance, most gun owners support the assault weapon ban and the Brady Act, which incorporates a waiting period and background checks. Also, both registering and limiting gun purchases are widely supported even by many gun owners (46). Clearly, many Americans support a variety of forms of limited gun control.

Parenthetical reference includes only page number when author already identified in transition

Paraphrase to support topic sentence with parenthetical reference identifying source

Topic sentence developing thesis idea

Transition identifying author and title

Only page number needed in parentheses

Extended paraphrase to support topic sentence

As much as many opponents of gun control would like to think otherwise, even the Second Amendment does not prohibit the control of firearms. In "Gun Control Is Constitutional," Robert Goldwin argues that the amendment is not a road block to gun control, but "a solid constitutional basis for effective national legislation to regulate guns and gun owners" (839). According to Goldwin, the First Congress of the United States, which authored the Second Amendment, saw that ordinary citizens needed to be able to defend themselves against national armies. In order to have such a defense, members of Congress agreed that there needed to be militias that could be called upon. And because there was a need for

Buyayo   3

militias, the right to carry guns was needed to keep them armed. Goldwin points out that this right to carry guns is protected by the first clause of the Second Amendment, which refers to "a well-regulated Militia" and that the Militia Act of 1792 required every white male citizen of the United States to enroll in the militia just in case of need (841). Everyone in the militia— which was similar to today's National Guard— was issued either a rifle or a musket and was given the complementary ammunition, and thus the citizens' need to protect themselves was met. However, as Goldwin makes clear, the government's need for a type of gun control was also met, in that whoever was issued the rifle or musket was also "enrolled" in the militia (841).

There are, of course, very practical reasons for controlling gun ownership. Without gun control, for instance, it would obviously be much easier for criminals to acquire guns. Opponents of gun control argue that criminals do not get guns "through customary retail channels" anyway (Wright 67), yet it is nevertheless true that every little bit of effort to keep guns from criminals will help. We must take measures to keep guns out of the wrong hands. We cannot let just anyone purchase a gun. In fact, just as some drugs are legal and some are illegal, guns must be regulated to make it difficult for criminals to use guns and for would-be criminals to buy guns. Furthermore, gun control will benefit our country in fiscal matters. According to John A. Calhoun in <u>Nation's Cities Weekly</u>, as a result of gun-related injuries, " . . . the public pays for wheelchairs, prosthetic devices, and, in some cases, a lifetime of care" (11). Calhoun goes on to say that such injuries cost the public more than $1.4 billion and more than $19 billion in productive lives (11).

Another reason why we need gun control is to prevent such tragedies as the Jonesboro shootings in Arkansas. These

[margin notes: Page references supplied for paraphrase; Topic sentence developing thesis idea; Parenthetical reference includes last name of author if author not identified in transition; Ellipsis needed when it is not obvious words have been omitted; Topic sentence developing thesis idea]

shootings were "terrible enough to warrant waking the President of the United States at midnight on his visit to Africa"

Parenthetical
references needed
for paraphrases

(Labi 29). In the city of Jonesboro, Arkansas, Drew Golden and Mitchell Johnson, 11 and 13 respectively, shot and killed four young girls and their teacher. Golden and Johnson had acquired guns that had been left unsecured (Labi 32). Gun control can help to prevent such tragedies in the future. In this case, child access prevention (CAP) would be the path to take. CAP laws require that parents be held responsible if they allow guns into a child's possession (Faltermayer 37). Although some people, such as Barry Krisberg, president of the National Council on Crime and Delinquency in San Francisco, have questioned the effectiveness of CAP laws, a study published in the Journal of the American Medical Association says that unintentional deaths in states that have enacted such laws have dropped 23 percent among children younger than 15 years old. (Faltermayer 37). California and Massachusetts, both of which have CAP laws, were awarded a "B" grade by Handgun Inc, a group that lobbies for gun control, for their success in keeping guns out of the hands of juveniles. The same group awarded Arkansas a "D" grade (Faltermayer 37).

Gun control is a highly controversial topic. Yes, our constitution provides real protection for gun owners, yet guns must be regulated. If we are willing to regulate something as necessary to modern living as car ownership, requiring that drivers attend driving schools, take tests, and have a license and insurance, certainly it is reasonable to regulate gun ownership too. Americans want gun control, for their own safety and the safety of others.

Buyayo 5

New page for
Works Cited

Sources listed
alphabetically by
last name

Second and
subsequent lines
indented 5 spaces

Article from
computerized
database

Article from a
weekly magazine

Article from a
collection

Author not known

Article from
monthly magazine

Works Cited

Blendon, Robert J., et al. "The American Public and the Gun
     Control Debate." The Journal of the American Medical Asso-
     ciation 275 (1996): 1719–1723. Expanded Academic ASAP.
     A 18395304. Information Access. 16 May 1998.

Calhoun, John A. "We Can Prevent Jonesboros." Nation's Cities
     Weekly April 1998: 11. Expanded Academic ASAP. A
     2051838. Information Access. 16 May 1998.

Faltermayer, Charlotte. "What Is Justice for a Sixth-Grade
     Killer?" Time 6 April 1998: 36–37.

Goldwin, Robert. "Gun Control Is Constitutional." Conversa-
     tions: Readings for Writing. Ed. Jack Selzer. Boston: Allyn
     and Bacon, 1997. 839–842.

Labi, Nadya. "The Jonesboro Shootings: The Hunter and the
     Choirboy." Time 6 April 1998: 27–36.

"Poll Shows Americans Split over Gun Safety Issues." American
     Medical News 39 (1996): 46. Expanded Academic ASAP. A
     18382323. Information Access. 16 May 1998.

Wright, James D. "Ten Essential Observations on Guns in
     America." Society March-April 1995: 63+.

EDITING YOUR PAPERS

COMPLETE SENTENCES

VERBS

PRONOUNS

MODIFIERS

PUNCTUATION

MECHANICS

WORD CHOICE AND SPELLING

COMPLETE SENTENCES

Recognizing Complete Sentences

Every complete sentence must contain a subject and a verb *and* must express a complete idea.

Sentence	$\overset{\text{S}}{Amelia} \overset{\text{V}}{likes}\ salad\ and\ pasta.$
Sentence	$The\ \overset{\text{S}}{bus}\ \overset{\text{V}}{stopped}\ for\ the\ train.$
No sentence (no verb)	$A\ \overset{\text{S}}{tour}\ of\ the\ factory\ at\ 10{:}00.$
No sentence (incomplete idea)	$After\ the\ \overset{\text{S}}{car}\ \overset{\text{V}}{crashed}\ yesterday.$

Main Clauses

A group of words that contains at least one subject and one verb and that expresses a complete idea is called a main clause. *Every complete sentence contains at least one main clause.*

One main clause	$\overset{\text{S}}{Alfonso}\ \overset{\text{V}}{stood}\ by\ the\ door\ of\ the\ gym.$

Combining Main Clauses

- Sentences can combine main clauses by using a comma and one of the coordinating conjunctions: *and, but, or, for, nor, so, yet.*

Two main clauses	$The\ \overset{\text{S}}{computer}\ \overset{\text{V}}{was}\ quite\ expensive,\ but\ \overset{\text{S}}{Sue}\ \overset{\text{V}}{bought}\ it$ anyway.

- Sentences can also combine main clauses using semicolons. Often the semicolons are followed by one of these transitional expressions.

accordingly	for example	however
as a result	for instance	indeed
consequently	furthermore	in fact
first	hence	instead

likewise	next	therefore
meanwhile	otherwise	thus
moreover	second	unfortunately
nevertheless	still	

Two main
clauses

$$\overset{S \quad V}{\textit{The bull pawed at the ground;}} \; \overset{S \quad V}{\textit{it looked restless.}}$$

$$\overset{S \qquad V}{\textit{Erika recognized the thief;}} \; \overset{S \quad V}{\textit{however, she refused to}}$$
identify him.

Subordinate Clauses

Subordinate clauses are subject-verb combinations that begin with one of the following subordinating words:

Subordinating Conjunctions		*Relative Pronouns*	
after	so that	that	who(ever)
although	than	which	whom(ever)
as	though		
as if	unless	(and sometimes when or where)	
as long as	until		
because	when		
before	whenever		
even though	where		
if	wherever		
since	while		

Combining Main Clauses and Subordinate Clauses

Complete sentences may contain subordinate clauses *in addition to* main clauses. But a subordinate clause without a main clause is not a complete sentence. In the following sentences, the subordinate clauses are underlined.

After we finish the game, we'll meet for pizza.

I like the food at Bogart's Restaurant although I dislike the atmosphere there.

Sarah, whom Ellis met at graduate school, was studying criminology.

EXERCISE

Underline all main clauses once and all subordinate clauses twice.

1. Environmental agencies like the Environmental Protection Agency are having an impact on our neighborhood.

2. For instance, I have noticed an electrical car that someone is driving around my small village.

3. Auto companies like Ford and Honda are developing electrical cars because the government has set a deadline for their introduction.

4. These cars are supposed to decrease the use of gasoline, which pollutes the environment.

5. The electrical cars are very quiet; therefore, they decrease noise pollution also.

6. Some of the cars are all electric, but some of them have a small fuel-burning engine in addition to the electric one.

7. Environmental laws have also caused an increase in the coyotes and raccoons in my neighborhood.

8. Although these animals sometimes get into garbage cans and bother family pets, our lives are richer for their presence.

9. The birds in our area have increased in number and variety because pesticide use has decreased.

10. People have mixed feelings about environmental groups like the Sierra Club and the EPA; however, I can see only benefits from their actions.

SENTENCE FRAGMENTS

A sentence fragment is an incomplete sentence. Because we often speak in partial sentences, it is easy to accidentally punctuate an incomplete sentence as if it were a complete sentence.

Types of Sentence Fragments

- Some fragments do not contain a subject and/or a verb.

  This kind of fragment is easy to spot. It usually does not even sound like a sentence.

  (fragment)   *The bird on the limb.*

  (fragment)   *The man from Brazil.*

  (sentence) $\overset{\text{S}}{We}\ \overset{\text{V}}{stared}$ *at the bird on the limb.*

  (sentence)   *The man from Brazil fainted in the airport.*
           S   V

- Some fragments contain an *-ing* verbal instead of a verb.

  Words ending in *-ing* are verb forms, but they are not used as verbs unless they follow helping verbs. By themselves, *running, eating, sleeping* are not verbs, but *is running, are eating, have been sleeping* are verbs.

  (fragment)   *The bird sitting on the limb.*

  (fragment)   *A woman walking quickly down the street.*

  (sentence)   *The bird sat on limb.*
               S V

  (sentence)   *A woman walking quickly down the street signaled for a taxi.*
           S   V

- Some fragments repeat a noun from a previous sentence.

  Don't punctuate a repeated noun as a separate sentence. Instead, use a comma to combine it with the noun it repeats.

      (sentence)   (repeated noun fragment)

  *Albert stared at the **building**. An old brick **church** on the corner.*

                           (sentence)

  *Albert stared at the **building**, an old brick **church** on the corner.*

- Some fragments contain a subordinate clause but no main clause.

  This is perhaps the most common fragment because subordinate clauses do have subjects and verbs. Remember, however, that all complete sentences must contain at least one *main clause.*

	(subordinate clause)
(fragment)	*While the bird sat on the limb.*

	(subordinate clause)
(fragment)	*Although the bird landed on the limb.*

	(main clause) (subordinate clause)
(sentence)	*The cat crept forward while the bird sat on the limb.*

	(subordinate clause) (main clause)
(sentence)	*Although the bird saw the cat, it did not fly away.*

Fixing Sentence Fragments

Once you have identified a fragment, you can fix it in one of two ways.

- Rewrite the fragment so that it contains a main clause.

(fragment)	*The bird sitting on the limb.*
(sentence)	*The bird <u>was</u> sitting on the limb.*
(fragment)	*While the bird sat on the limb.*
(sentence)	*While the bird sat on the limb, <u>Maria looked at it with her binoculars.</u>*

- Combine the fragment with a sentence written before or after it.

(incorrect)	*I could not avoid the thunderstorm. <u>A frightening combination of lightning bolts and hail.</u>*
(correct)	*I could not avoid the thunderstorm, a frightening combination of lightning bolts and hail.*
(incorrect)	*Maria could not see the birds in the trees. <u>Because she did not have her binoculars with her.</u>*
(correct)	*Maria could not see the birds in the trees because she did not have her binoculars with her.*

EXERCISE

Correct any sentence fragments.

1. Andrea enjoyed listening to John Coltrane. A jazz saxophonist whom she had admired for a long time.

2. Because he seemed to put so much sincere emotion into his music, *it looked as though every note came from the heart.*

3. She followed his career. *seeing* Going to see him at every opportunity.

4. In his early years he had played with several great musicians. Especially as a member of a group with Miles Davis.

5. That group included another great sax player, *by the name of* Cannonball Adderly.

6. Later, Coltrane went out on his own, And formed a quartet.

7. This group included the pianist McCoy Tyner. Elvin Jones played the drums. *and Elvin Jones, who plays the drums,*

8. The group was famous for renditions of songs like "My Favorite Things," Because the solos on these songs were so creative.

9. Andrea admired the songs John Coltrane wrote himself, *mainly* Her special favorites being "Alabama" and "After the Rain."

10. When Andrea traveled to Japan for Coltrane's tour there, She saw him play some of his most experimental and creative music, like "A Love Supreme."

Run-on Sentences

Run-on sentences are major grammatical errors that come in two types: **fused sentences** and **comma splices**. They both occur for the same reason—two main clauses are joined without the proper punctuation or coordinating conjunction.

Fused Sentences

A fused sentence occurs when two or more main clauses are joined without a coordinating conjunction or punctuation.

	(main clause)	(main clause)
(fused)	*Jorge read the newspaper*	*then he wrote a letter.*

	(main clause)	(main clause)
(fused)	*The day was cloudy*	*it looked like rain.*

	(main clause)	(main clause)
(fused)	*The house was deserted*	*Marty decided to enter it*

anyway.

Comma Splices

The comma splice is similar to the fused sentence except that a comma appears between the two main clauses. A comma splice occurs when two or more main clauses are joined by only a comma.

	(main clause)	(,)	(main clause)
(comma splice)	*The fifteenth inning began,*		*it was already midnight.*

A comma splice also occurs when a writer joins two main clauses with a comma and a transitional word or phrase rather than with a semicolon and a transitional word or phrase.

	(main clause)	(, transition)	(main clause)
(comma splice)	*Juanita was hungry,*	*however,*	*it was still two hours until*

lunch time.

	(main clause)	(, transition)
(comma splice)	*The sand was warm and soothing,*	*on the other hand,*

(main clause)
the surf was quite rough.

Fixing Fused Sentences and Comma Splices

Fused sentences and comma splices can be fixed in the same five ways. Consider these two errors:

| (fused) | *The hikers saw the grizzly bear they were afraid.* |
| (comma splice) | *The hikers saw the grizzly bear, they were afraid.* |

Both errors can be fixed in one of five ways:

- Punctuate the two clauses as separate sentences.
  The hikers saw the grizzly bear. They were afraid.
- Join the two clauses with a comma and a coordinating conjunction.
  The hikers saw the grizzly bear, and they were afraid.
- Join the two clauses with a semicolon.
  The hikers saw a grizzly bear; they were afraid.
- Join the two clauses with a semicolon and a transitional word or phrase.
  (See pages 69–70 for a list of common transitions.)
  The hikers saw a grizzly bear; as a result, they were afraid.
- Make one of the clauses a subordinate clause.
  When the hikers saw a grizzly bear, they were afraid.

EXERCISE

Correct any fused sentences and comma splices.

1. Recently, some older fashions and fads have returned they are not especially attractive ones.
2. One of them is platform shoes; however, this time even sneakers have heels and soles up to three inches thick.
3. These shoes are not just unattractive, they might even be dangerous.
4. Many people who wear them walk unsteadily they look as if they have been drinking.
5. In addition, bell bottoms have reappeared; at least when they were worn by sailors, they had some practical purpose.
6. Bell bottoms do not flatter the physique of the wearer, nevertheless, they are a popular clothing item lately.
7. Yo-yos have also returned the hula hoop should reappear soon.

8. Then one could yo-yo and hula hoop at the same time; wearing platform sneakers and bell bottoms would complete the look.

9. Perhaps these old fashions reflect a nostalgia for the twentith century; there might not be any specific reason for their popularity.

10. Maybe leisure suits will come back; we might even see some tie-dyed shirts.

SUBJECT-VERB AGREEMENT

Subject-verb agreement means that the verb you use in a sentence must match the subject. If your subject is singular, your verb must be singular. If your subject is plural, your verb must be plural.

Problem Areas

Almost all subject-verb agreement errors occur for one of two reasons: Either the writer has identified the wrong word as the subject, or the writer thinks a subject is singular when it is really plural (or vice versa). The following points address these two problems.

- Subjects are never part of a prepositional phrase.

  Prepositional phrases often occur between the subject and the verb. Do not confuse the object of the prepositional phrase with the subject of the verb.

    S   V

  One of the students walks to school

  The subject is *One,* not *students,* because *students* is part of the prepositional phrase *of the students.*

  Here is a list of common prepositions to help you identify prepositional phrases:

about	because of	except	of	toward
above	before	for	on	under
across	behind	from	onto	until
after	below	in	over	up
among	beside	in spite of	past	upon
around	between	into	through	with
as	by	like	till	without
at	during	near	to	

- In a sentence that begins with *there* or *here,* the order of the subject and verb is reversed.

         V   S

  *There **were** several **people** in the park this morning.*

   V   S
Here is the person with the keys.

- Only the subject affects the form of the verb.

            S   V
His most important fear was the elephants charging toward him.

The singular verb form is correct here because the subject is the singular noun *fear*. The plural noun *elephants* does not affect the form of the verb.

- Two subjects joined by *and* are plural.

   S   S   V
The wagon and the chair were for sale.

   S   S   V
The power and the water appear to be out.

- If a subject is modified by *each* or *every,* it is singular.

     S   S   V
Each marine and soldier was responsible for a section of the beach.

     S   S   V
Every runner and spectator is eager for the start.

- Indefinite pronouns are usually singular.

  S   V
Each of the horses has a handler.

  S   V
Everybody in the auditorium was a member of the club.

- A few nouns and indefinite pronouns, such as *none, some, all, most, more, half,* or *part* (and other fractions), may sometimes be considered plural and sometimes singular, depending on the prepositional phrase that follows them.

         S   V
(singular)   *Half of the milk is non-fat.*

         S   V
(plural)   *Half of the stores were open.*

- When *either/or, neither/nor, not only/but also,* or just *or* joins the subjects, the verb agrees with the subject closer to it.

       S   S   V
Neither the bear nor the tigers want to enter the enclosure.

If you reverse the order of the subjects above, you must change the verb form.

         S   S   V
*Neither the **tigers** nor the **bear wants** to leave the enclosure.*

- Collective nouns usually take the singular form of the verb. Collective nouns represent groups of people or things, but they are considered singular. Some common collective nouns are *audience, band, class, committee, crowd, family, flock, group, herd, jury, society,* and *team.*

       S   V
*The **class was asked** to leave the room quickly.*

       S   V
*The **team runs** twenty laps at the end of practice.*

- A few nouns end in "s" but are considered singular; they take the singular form of the verb. These nouns include *economics, gymnastics, mathematics, measles, mumps, physics,* and *politics.*

     S   V
Physics is not my favorite subject.

       S   V
*The **news was** unusual tonight.*

- When units of measurement for distance, time, volume, height, weight, money, and so on are used as subjects, they take the singular verb form.

     S   V
*Five gallons of water **was** all that we needed.*

     S   V
*Forty miles **is** a long hike.*

EXERCISE

Correct any subject-verb agreement errors.

1. Our choice of movies ~~have~~ has become interesting in recent years.
2. Disaster in many forms seem to be on people's minds.
3. One of the most popular and expensive of disaster films have been *Titanic.*
4. *Titanic,* along with other contemporary films, ~~were~~ was very successful at the box office.

5. Are the movie industry or today's audiences fearful because a millennium is ending?

6. *Independence Day* and *Armageddon* presents stories about the world being destroyed.

7. In addition to these, there is disaster movies such as *Sudden Impact, Volcano,* and *Twister.*

8. Each of these movies play on our fears about impending danger.

9. Every viewer, young or old, have different reasons for seeing these films.

10. These movies all have one thing in common: the audience want to be thrilled.

CONSISTENCY IN VERB TENSE

Verb tenses indicate whether an action happened in the past, present, or future. Sometimes writers accidentally shift from one tense to another when there is no reason to do so. Such unnecessary shifts occur most commonly between the past and present tenses.

Don't Shift Between Past and Present Tenses Without Reason

(unnecessary shift)   *When Joel* ***saw*** ^{past} *the lion at the circus yesterday, he* ***sits*** ^{present}

right in front of its cage and ***starts*** ^{present} *to tease it.*

(necessary shift)   *Alex* ***hopes*** ^{present} *that he* ***will win*** ^{future} *tonight's lottery because last*

weekend he ***lost*** ^{past} *all of his rent money in Las Vegas.*

Don't Leave Off the *-d* or *-ed* Endings in Past Tense Verbs

If you do not pronounce the *-d* or *-ed* endings when you speak, you might mistakenly leave them off when you write. If you are discussing an event that occurred in the past, add *-d* or *-ed* where such endings are needed.

(incorrect)   *After the party last night, Mark* ***thank*** *Fiona for giving him a ride home.*

(correct)   *After the party last night, Mark* ***thanked*** *Fiona for giving him a ride home.*

Don't Leave Off the *-d* Ending in *supposed to* or *used to*

(incorrect)   *Phung is* ***suppose to*** *be on a diet, but he can't get* ***use to*** *skipping his usual dessert of chocolate chip ice cream.*

(correct)   *Phung is* ***supposed to*** *be on a diet, but he can't get* ***used to*** *skipping his usual dessert of chocolate chip ice cream.*

Use Present Tense When Discussing Someone Else's Writing

Use the present tense when you write about someone else's writing—whether non-fiction, fiction, or poetry—or when you write about film. Don't mistakenly shift to the past tense.

(incorrect)   *In "Why I Won't Buy My Sons Toy Guns," Robert Shaffer **claims** toys are teachers. He **said** that toy guns will teach children to solve problems with violence.*

(correct)   *In "Why I Won't Buy My Sons Toy Guns," Robert Shaffer **claims** toys are teachers. He **says** that toy guns will teach children to solve problems with violence.*

EXERCISE

Correct any verb tense problems.

1. Supposedly when Hemingway wrote his novels, he decide to compose just one hundred precise words each day.
2. Later in his life, after he was severely injured in a plane crash, he stands at his typewriter and composes those words.
3. My professors use to point out that he used almost no adjectives.
4. Dr. Hibbard, my Hemingway professor, would come into the classroom, and he then sits on his desk and goes over each Hemingway novel or story almost one word at a time.
5. His favorite story is "Cat in the Rain," which was only about two pages long.
6. Hemingway has been describe as insensitive in his depiction of women.
7. But he writes "Cat in the Rain" convincingly from the point of view of a woman.
8. The story was about a husband and wife who are visiting a foreign country.
9. The story revealed just a few details about the couple, and we are suppose to draw inferences from those details.
10. When I was in class, Professor Hibbard sits at his desk with the book open and tells us the significance of each detail.

CONSISTENCY IN VERB VOICE

Identifying Active Voice and Passive Voice

Verb "voice" refers to the relationship between the subject and the verb of a sentence. If the subject is performing or "doing" the verb, the sentence is in **active** voice. If the subject is receiving the action of the verb, the sentence is in **passive** voice. Note that the subject is the "doer" in the following active voice sentence:

S   V

(active voice)   *A red-tailed hawk seized the unsuspecting rabbit.*
(The subject—the hawk—<u>performs</u> the action.)

Now, compare the above active voice sentence with its passive voice counterpart:

S   V

(passive voice)   *The unsuspecting rabbit was seized by a red-tailed hawk.*
(The subject—the rabbit—<u>receives</u> the action.)

Choosing the Active Voice

Most writers prefer the active voice. It is more direct than passive voice, and it uses fewer words. In fact, too many passive voice verbs can make your writing sound dull and lifeless. Active voice also identifies who or what is performing the action. Passive voice, on the other hand, often obscures the "doer" of the action. Who, for example, denied the building permit in the following sentence?

(passive voice)   *After serious consideration, your request for a building permit **has been denied**.*

(active voice)   *After serious consideration, **the members of the city council have voted** to deny your request for a building permit.*

Choosing the Passive Voice

Although most writers prefer the active voice, the passive voice does have a place in good writing, particularly in the following situations.

• Use passive voice when the performer of an action is unimportant or when the receiver of the action needs to be emphasized.

S   V

*All of the buildings **had been inspected** by noon yesterday.*
(Who did the inspecting is not important.)

- Use passive voice when the performer of the action is unknown.

      S V

*Last night my car **was stolen** from the Wal-Mart parking lot.*
(Who stole the car is not known.)

- Use passive voice when the receiver of the action needs to be emphasized.

         S   V

*During the Holocaust Jewish **people were executed** by the hundreds of thousands.*
(The receiver of the action—Jewish people—is being emphasized.)

Changing Passive Voice to Active Voice

Some people write too many passive voice sentences merely because they can't figure out how to change them to the active voice. Use these suggestions to revise your passive sentences to active ones.

- If the performer of the action is an object (objects usually follow the verb), reverse the subject and the object.

            S   O

(passive voice) *The CD ROM drive was purchased by John for $200.*

            S   O

(active voice) *John purchased the CD ROM drive for $200.*

- If the performer of the action has been left out of the sentence, write it in as the subject.

             S   V

(passive voice) *Every official transcript was destroyed last night.*

           S V

(active voice) *Last night's fire destroyed every official transcript.*

- Change the verb.

            V

(passive voice) *Stephen Spielberg was given an Academy award for directing <u>Schindler's List.</u>*

V

(active voice)   *Stephen Spielberg received an Academy award for directing <u>Schindler's List.</u>*

EXERCISE

Change passive voice verbs to the active voice.

1. A few years ago Darby, an Australian Shepherd, was bought from a breeder by my family.
2. She was chosen by us from a litter of ten.
3. In Australia, sheep and cattle were once herded by dogs like Darby.
4. Before she was brought to our home, Darby was taken to get her shots.
5. We were told by the breeder to keep newspapers on the laundry room floor for the first few days.
6. After a while, it was decided by my daughter that Darby should learn to catch a Frisbee.
7. Within a week, a Frisbee could be caught and returned by our new pet.
8. Whenever a new trick was learned by Darby, she was rewarded by us with a treat.
9. For fun Darby was sometimes called names like "Darbaloney," "Darbinger," "Darboney," or "Miss Darby" by my daughter Michelle.
10. These days we are accompanied by Darby wherever we go.

Pronoun Agreement

Because a pronoun takes the place of a noun, it must match or "agree with" the noun that it replaces.

The Informal *You*

Restrict the use of the word *you* to informal writing, personal letters, and instructions. Most college papers require a more formal approach. Be especially careful not to use *you* if you are writing *about* other people rather than *to* them.

(incorrect)	Most **users** of word processing programs will be successful if **you** follow the directions in the manual.
(correct)	Most **users** of word processing programs will be successful if **they** follow the directions in the manual.

Singular Versus Plural Pronouns

- Use a plural pronoun to refer to words joined by *and*.

  William Shakespeare and Sophocles are both famous for **their** tragedies.

- Use singular pronouns to refer to the following indefinite pronouns.

one	anybody	everybody	nobody	somebody
each	anyone	everyone	no one	someone
either	anything	everything	nothing	something
neither				

Everyone on the team was proud of **her** work.
Neither of the pilots wanted to abandon **his** plane.
One of the giant pandas was pulling at the bamboo with **its** paws.

In spoken English, the plural pronouns *they, them* and *their* are often used to refer to the antecedents *everyone* or *everybody*. However, in written English the singular pronoun is still more commonly used.

Everybody on the debate team determined to do **his** best.

- Use singular pronouns to refer to collective nouns. Some common collective nouns are *audience, band, class, committee, crowd, family, flock, group, herd, jury, society,* and *team.*

  The *family* departed on *its* annual trip to Yosemite.

  The *company* has *its* picnic for the families in October.

- When words are joined by *or, nor, either/or, neither/nor,* or *not only/ but also,* the pronoun should agree with the word closer to it.

  Neither *Shirley* nor the other tennis *players* brought *their* extra racquets.

  The plural pronoun *their* agrees with the plural noun *players* because *players* is the closer noun.

Pronouns and Sexist Language

Many singular nouns and pronouns can be either masculine or feminine. (Consider, for example, the nouns *doctor, student, person,* or *teacher* or the pronouns *everyone, someone,* or *no one.*) In the past it was traditional to use masculine pronouns when referring to such nouns, but many people find that tradition offensive today. Consider the following approaches to this problem.

- Use a plural noun rather than a singular one.

Rather than this:	*An **officer** should be careful whenever **he** approaches a driver's window.*
Try this:	***Officers** should be careful whenever **they** approach a driver's window.*

- Use feminine pronouns as well as masculine ones to refer to gender-free nouns.

  *An **officer** should be careful whenever **she** approaches a driver's window.*

- Use *he or she.* (But this solution is quite awkward. Use it sparingly.)

  *An **officer** should be careful whenever **he or she** approaches a driver's window.*

- Rewrite the sentence without using a pronoun:

  *An **officer** should be careful whenever approaching a driver's window.*

EXERCISE

Correct any errors in pronoun agreement.

1. When a person enters our town's new cybermall, you will be impressed by its extensive use of technology.

2. Everyone who enters is given their very own mini-computer.

3. When people check out the mini-computer, he or she has to leave an ID like a driver's license.

4. The company that developed the mall has done their job well.

5. Both individuals and family groups can easily find their way around with the aid of the computers.

6. Mr. Silicon, the manager, tells new customers that you would enjoy a meal at the Technomat, a restaurant that just opened.

7. Someone once told me that they love the coffee at the Technomat.

8. Either Mr. Silicon or his assistant Mr. Byte will offer their assistance to anyone who wants to open a new store in the cybermall.

9. The mini-computers show people who are using it what is in each store and how to get there.

10. Last Saturday, our family thoroughly enjoyed their visit to the cybermall.

PRONOUN REFERENCE

Write Pronouns So That They Clearly Refer to a Specific Word

(unclear)   *When the coach told Tony the bad news, he began to cry.*
             (Who began to cry? Perhaps the coach did.)

(clear)   *When the coach told Tony the bad news, Tony began to cry.*

(clear)   *When the coach told him the bad news, Tony began to cry.*

Use the Pronouns *Which, This, That,* and *It* with Care

❖ **Which**

Which is often used in ways that are confusing. If the word or idea it refers to is not clear, rewrite the sentence without using *which*.

(unclear)   *My daughter practices golf nearly every day, which I really don't like.*
             (What don't I like? Golf? My daughter's constant practicing?)

(clear)   *My daughter practices golf nearly every day. I really don't like her practicing that often.*

❖ **This**

This should refer to specific word, not to a vague or general idea. Use a noun after the pronoun *this* to clarify its meaning.

(unclear)   *We were not seated even though we had stood in line for five hours. This was beginning to frustrate us.*

(clear)   *We were not seated even though we had stood in line for five hours. This long wait was beginning to frustrate us.*

❖ **That**

That often has the same problem as *this*. Use a noun after *that* when doing so clarifies your meaning.

(unclear)   *Chang's back stopped hurting, and then he won $150 in*

*Las Vegas. **That** really cheered him up.*

(clear) *Chang's back stopped hurting, and then he won $150 in Las Vegas. **That extra money** really cheered him up.*

❖ **It**

Use *it* carefully. Rewrite the sentence if what *it* refers to is confusing or unclear.

(unclear) *On the news it said that the hurricane was approaching Miami.*

(clear) *The weather report on the news said that the hurricane was approaching Miami.*

EXERCISE

Correct any errors in pronoun reference.

1. General Beauregard and General Lee were discussing his horse. *[their horses,]*
2. General Lee's horse Traveller needed attention, ~~but~~ the battle was ~~about to start, which~~ worried General Lee. *[and starting battle.]*
3. General Pickett thought that a blacksmith should look at Traveller because the horse acted lame, and that is what General Lee did. *[General Lee followed his instructions]*
4. When Pickett showed Lee his new horse, he smiled. *[Lee]*
5. Pickett's horse looked like the one Lee had ridden at West Point. This made Lee remember his student days. *[Pickett's horse]*
6. Lee's horse, Traveller, was led up to Pickett's horse, and it started jumping around. *[Traveller they]*
7. In the report that Pickett read, ~~it~~ said that Gettysburg could be easily taken.
8. Pickett and Lee discussed the best way that he could attack the Union forces. *[they]*
9. Pickett's wife talked to Lee's mother ~~because she~~ was worried about her son. *[Pickett's wife]*
10. Over forty thousand soldiers were killed or wounded at the Battle of Gettysburg, and this was a turning point in the war. *[B of Gettysburg]*

PRONOUN CASE

Pronouns appear in a variety of spellings, depending on how they are being used in a sentence. For example, to refer to yourself you can use *I, me, my, mine,* or *myself.* These different spellings are the result of what is called pronoun case.

Using *I* or *me, we* or *us, he* or *him, she* or *her, they* or *them*

- Use *I, we, he, she,* and *they* when the pronoun is a subject.

  S
  I am fond of peanut butter.

  S
  They are after me.

- Use *I, we, he, she,* and *they* after linking verbs (*am, are, is, was, were*).

  It was she who broke the record.

  The winner of the last race is he.

- If sentences like the last two sound awkward and stilted to you, revise them so the pronoun is the subject of the sentence.

  She broke the record.

  He is the winner of the last race.

- Use *me, us, him, her,* and *them* when the pronoun is an object (that is, when it receives the action of the verb or when it is part of a prepositional phrase).

  Emilia asked him about the handkerchief.

  Antonio drove me to the airport.

  Scott wondered if Zelda had sent the note to him.

  Homer bought her some okra perfume.

Paired Words (*Joe and I* or *Joe and me*)

To decide which spelling of a pronoun to use in paired words, drop out the other words in the pair and use only the pronoun. Do not be afraid to use *me* in paired words. *I* is not always the correct choice.

(paired words) **Homer and <u>she</u> milked the cows.**
(*She* milked the cows.)

(paired words) **The boy sold the puppies to my father and <u>me.</u>**
(The boy sold the puppies to *me*)

(paired words) **Last night my boss fired Hyun and <u>me.</u>**
(Last night my boss fired *me*.)

Who and *Whom*

To choose between *who* and *whom,* remember these points:

- Use *who* when it is the subject of the subordinate clause. Use *whom* when some other word is the subject of the subordinate clause.

         S   V
*Paul saw a man **<u>who looked like an undercover police officer</u>***
(*Who* is the subject of the subordinate clause.)

         S   V
*The person **<u>whom we choose for the prize</u>** will be happy.*
(*We* is the subject of the subordinate clause.)

- Use *who* when it is the subject of the question. Use *whom* when some other word is the subject of the question. (In conversation, *who* is often used in place of *whom*.)

  S   V
***Who** is knocking at the door?*
(*Who* is the subject of the question.)

      V   S   V
***Whom** did you see at the concert?*
(*You* is the subject of the question.)

Comparisons

When a pronoun is used in a comparison, decide which form to use by supplying the implied words. The implied words directly repeat part of the sentence.

For example, in the following sentence the implied words are *can play back-gammon:*

(without implied words)   *My cousin can play backgammon better than I.*

(with implied words)   *My cousin can play backgammon better than I* [can play backgammon].

(without implied words)   *At dinner my father gave my brother more turkey than* **me.**

(with implied words)   *At dinner my father gave my brother more turkey than* [my father gave] **me.**

Using *myself, ourselves, yourself, yourselves, himself, herself, itself, themselves*

- Use a *-self* or *-selves* pronoun only when no other pronoun will work.

(incorrect)   *Marie wondered if Alma and* **herself** *should leave.*

(correct)   *Marie wondered if Alma and* **she** *should leave.*

(correct)   *The owner of the salon put out the fire by* **himself.**

- Don't use non-standard spelling of *-self* or *-selves* pronouns.

(incorrect)   *The two children laughed when they saw* **theirselves** *in the mirror.*

(correct)   *The two children laughed when they saw* **themselves** *in the mirror.*

(incorrect)   *We decided to paint the house by* **ourself.**

(correct)   *We decided to paint the house by* **ourselves.**

EXERCISE

Correct any errors in pronoun case.

1. My professor and me were discussing Tony Hillerman.
2. It was her who introduced me to my first Tony Hillerman novel.
3. One of the differences between her and I is that she is from the South and I am from the Southwest.
4. My professor, whom is from Alabama, became interested in Tony Hillerman when she moved to New Mexico.

5. In fact, she knows more about the settings of Hillerman's novels than me, even though I was born in Arizona and lived in New Mexico.

6. Both the professor and myself enjoy Hillerman's main characters, Jim Chee and Joe Leaphorn.

7. In the novels, Chee and Leaphorn are always involving theirselfs in solving crimes around the Four Corners area.

8. For ourselfs, the Native American lore and customs are the most interesting parts of the novels.

9. Because she is an expert on the history of the Southwest, she knows much more than me about these customs.

10. When Tony Hillerman came to town, he signed his books for the professor and I.

MISPLACED MODIFIERS

When a modifier is misplaced, it seems to describe or refer to a word that it is not meant to describe or refer to. Consider the following sentence, for example:

> *The pastor asked them **quietly** to move into the chapel.*

Does the modifier *quietly* state how the pastor asked them, or does it state how they were supposed to move into the chapel? Changing the placement of the modifier will clarify the meaning.

> *The pastor **quietly** asked them to move into the chapel.*
> (Here the word modifies the verb *asked.*)

> The pastor asked them to move *quietly* into the chapel.
> (Here the word modifies the infinitive *to move.*)

Misplaced Words (*only, almost, just, nearly, merely*)

Place these five words carefully. Usually they precede the words they modify.

(misplaced)	*Alfredo **almost** drank a gallon of lemonade today.*
(correct)	*Alfredo drank **almost** a gallon of lemonade today.* (*Almost* modifies *a gallon,* not *drank,* so it precedes *a gallon.*)
(misplaced)	*At today's sale, Cecilia **only** saved five dollars on her mountain bicycle.*
(correct)	*At today's sale, Cecilia saved **only** five dollars on her mountain bicycle.* (*Only* modifies *five dollars,* not *saved,* so it precedes *five dollars.*)

Misplaced Phrases and Clauses

Generally, phrases and clauses should appear immediately before or after the words they modify.

(misplaced)	*A tall man stepped in front of the car **with a cowboy hat on.***
(correct)	*A tall man **with a cowboy hat on** stepped in front of the car.*

(misplaced)	*The actor stroked her cat **trying to memorize her lines.***
(correct)	*The actor **trying to memorize her lines** stroked her cat.*
(misplaced)	*Sam gave the shirts to his little brother **that he had outgrown.***
(correct)	*Sam gave the shirts **that he had outgrown** to his little brother.*
(misplaced)	*They returned the chair to the factory **missing two legs.***
(correct)	*They returned the chair **missing two legs** to the factory.*

EXERCISE

Revise the sentences to correctly place any misplaced modifiers.

1. The psychologist told us carefully to watch the presentation on road rage.
2. He only spoke for a minute before he showed us a tape.
3. A driver with a toy poodle talking on a cellular phone became angry with an old woman who was crossing a busy street.
4. The car with the angry driver spinning out of control missed the woman by only six inches.
5. The woman almost fainted when she realized how close the car had come.
6. In another instance, an English teacher driving a Ford pickup with a bad temper rammed a car that was going too slowly.
7. Infuriated, the driver responded with an insulting hand gesture who had been rammed.
8. The tail light of the driver smashed in the confrontation would not work.
9. The English teacher nearly drove twenty miles before he pulled over.
10. The drivers getting out of their cars quickly started fighting.

Dangling Modifiers

Recognizing Dangling Modifiers

Dangling modifiers usually occur at the start of a sentence. They "dangle" because they express an action that the subject of the sentence cannot perform.

(dangling)   *Trying to impress his boss, the joke was in bad taste.*
             (A *joke* cannot try to impress someone.)

(correct)   *Trying to impress his boss, Seymour told a tasteless joke.*
             (*Seymour* can try to impress someone.)

(dangling)   *Smiling at the results, the redecorating job was appreciated.*
             (A *job* cannot smile.)

(correct)   *Smiling at the results, Vincent appreciated the redecorating job.*
             (*Vincent* can smile.)

Correcting Dangling Modifiers

You can correct dangling modifiers in one of two ways.

* Rewrite the sentence so that it includes a subject that can perform the action of the modifier.

  (dangling)   *When attending the workshop, new techniques were learned.*
               (*Techniques* cannot attend workshops.)

  (correct)   *When attending the workshop, I learned new techniques.*
               (*I* attended the workshop.)

* Rewrite the dangling modifier so that it contains its own subject.

  (dangling)   *Stepping into the street, a car nearly hit me.*
               (A car cannot step into the street.)

  (correct)   *When I stepped into the street, a car nearly hit me.*
               (I can step into the street.)

What Not to Do

- Don't correct a dangling modifier by moving it to the end of the sentence. It still will not have a subject that can perform its action.

(dangling)   *After trying three times, the **test** still was not passed.*
    (The *test* cannot try three times.)

(still incorrect)   *The **test** still was not passed after trying three times.*
    (The *test* cannot try three times.)

- Don't correct a dangling modifier by adding a possessive noun or pronoun to the sentence. It still will not have a subject that can perform its action.

(still incorrect)   *After trying three times, **Cynthia's test** still was not passed.*
    (*Cynthia's test* cannot try three times.)

- Here are two possible corrections:

(correct)   *After trying three times, Cynthia **still had not passed the test.***
    (*Cynthia* can try three times.)

(correct)   *After **Cynthia** had tried three times, she still had not passed the test.*
    (*Cynthia* had tried three times.)

EXERCISE

Correct any dangling modifiers.

1. Slipping the disk into the drive, the icon appeared on the screen.
2. Hoping to make the machine faster, sixty-four megabytes of memory were added.
3. After installing the program, a large question mark appeared on the screen.
4. Hoping to be browsing the Internet soon, Hector double-clicked the icon.
5. Slowly assembling on the monitor screen, Jack could see the outlines of a scenic mountain range.
6. To get rid of the picture, he pressed the escape button.

7. Confused and irritated by the computer, Tasha's mouse clicked on one icon after another.

8. Finally seeing the logo for the Internet browser, Isaac jumped for joy.

9. Smiling broadly, the computer revealed Aaron's favorite site.

10. Satisfied at last that all was well, the game *Maladjusted Participles* was launched.

COMMAS

Comma use can be broken down into four general rules:

- Use commas before coordinating conjunctions that join main clauses.
- Use commas between elements in a series.
- Use commas after introductory elements.
- Use commas before and after interrupting elements.

Use a Comma before a Coordinating Conjunction That Joins Main Clauses

- Use a comma and a coordinating conjunction (*and, but, or, for, nor, so, yet*), to join two main clauses.

  Yosemite is a beautiful national park, and Yellowstone has its own special beauty too.

  Daedalus had to gather many feathers, or he would never be able to fly.

- Do not use a comma when a coordinating conjunction joins other parts of a sentence.

  Every day Charlie plays with his Barry Manilow album and then packs his two black satchels.

Use Commas between Elements in a Series

- Use commas to separate items in a series (a list). The comma before the last item is optional.

  The Cityfest Music Scene was exciting, stimulating, and crowded.

  Penelope wanted to redecorate the palace, to do some knitting, and to get rid of all of the men hanging around the palace.

- Use a comma to separate two or more adjectives that modify the same noun if you can put *and* between them or if you can easily reverse their order.

  Omar watched the fierce, determined warriors assault the fortress.

  The stormy, dark day was perfect for reading a mystery in front of the fire.

Note that you could use *and* between the adjectives. (The warriors are *fierce* and *determined*; the day is *stormy* and *dark*.) You could also reverse the adjectives (the *determined, fierce* warriors or the *dark, stormy* day).

Use a Comma after an Introductory Element

- Use a comma after transitional expressions such as *first, moreover, however, on the other hand, similarly, for example, as a result, in other words*.

Next, Penelope unraveled her knitting.
As a result, Charles refused to see his father.

- Use a comma after introductory phrases.

After the insufferably boring lecture, we decide to have coffee and chocolate mousse at the Rambeau Arms.
Flying higher than any bird, Icarus felt exhilarated.
Heated by the sun, the wax began to melt.

- Use a comma after a subordinate clause that precedes a main clause.

As the wax melted, the feathers began to fall.
Because he fell into the sea and drowned, Icarus has come to symbolize the over-reaching ambition of youth.

Use Commas to Set off Interrupting Elements

- Use a pair of commas to set off transitional expressions. Note that you need two commas—one before and one after each transitional expression.

A change in policy, therefore, was a necessity.
Pablo, on the other hand, preferred oil paints.

- Use a pair of commas to set off modifying phrases and clauses that interrupt the sentence. Modifiers interrupt the sentence if they are not needed to identify the word they modify.

(commas)   *The DC-3, which was an indispensable plane in World War II, is still in use in many parts of the world.*

(*Which was an indispensable plane in World War II* interrupts the sentence because it is not needed to identify the DC-3.)

(no commas)   *One of the generals <u>who won the Battle of the Bulge</u> was George Patton.*
(*Who won the Battle of the Bulge* does not interrupt the sentence because it is needed to identify which "general" you are referring to.)

(commas)   *The winner of the marathon, <u>breathing deeply and smiling at the crowd</u>, raised her right hand.*
(*Breathing deeply and smiling at the crowd* interrupts the sentence because it is not needed to identify the winner.)

(no commas)   *The plane <u>flying toward the lake</u> made a low droning sound.*
(*Flying toward the lake* is needed to identify the plane.)

(commas)   *Her novel, <u>the work of twenty years</u>, was finally published in March.*
(*The work of twenty years* interrupts the sentence because it is not needed to identify her novel.)

- Use a pair of commas to set off words of direct address. If a writer addresses someone directly in a sentence, the words that stand for that person or persons are set off by commas. If the words in direct address begin a sentence, they are followed by a comma.

Did you know, <u>Jack</u>, that you are constantly smiling these days?
<u>Bruce</u>, the best thing is just not to worry.
We'll dance one more dance, and then we'll go, <u>Suzie</u>.

- Use a pair of commas to set off dates and addresses. If your sentence contains two or more elements of a date or address, use commas to set off these elements.

On <u>Tuesday</u>, <u>November 21</u>, <u>1952</u>, we began our trip from Tennessee to Minnesota.
Darby lives at <u>3245 McKinley Street</u>, <u>Carlsbad</u>, <u>California 92008</u>, for the time being.
Note: The state is not separated from the zip code by a comma.

Exercise

Add commas where they are needed.

1. Originating in Greek mythology the story of Icarus and Daedalus has been interpreted in several ways.

2. According to the myth Daedalus and Icarus his son are imprisoned in the labyrinth that Daedalus has built.

3. The two men gather wax and feathers and Daedalus constructs wings for them.

4. Daedalus tells Icarus to gather more feathers wax and water before they leave.

5. My son first heard the story of Icarus from a waiter at the Feta Cheese Cafe 1416 James Joyce Way Dublin Ireland when he was ten years old.

6. Most versions of the myth claim that Daedalus warns Icarus not to fly near the hot sun.

7. Icarus unfortunately is an excitable boy so he does not obey.

8. Daedalus who is a very careful man does not fly close to the sun but Icarus is so excited that he flies higher and higher.

9. When Icarus gets close to the sun the wax on his wings melts the feathers fall off and he perishes in the sea.

10. Many parents say this myth is a lesson in disobedience but Anne Sexton a famous poet believes Icarus should be admired for his daring and exuberance.

SEMICOLONS

Use a Semicolon to Join Two Closely Related Main Clauses

- Join two main clauses with a semicolon to emphasize that they are closely related. Do *not* use a coordinating conjunction with the semicolon.

  He chose the blue Honda Accord; she preferred the green Toyota Camry.

  Cheryl covered half of the ice cream with chocolate sauce; the other half she covered with whipped cream.

- Semicolons that join main clauses are often followed by one of these transitional expressions:

accordingly	however	next
as a result	indeed	otherwise
consequently	in fact	second
first	instead	still
for example	likewise	therefore
for instance	meanwhile	thus
furthermore	moreover	unfortunately
hence	nevertheless	

  Gabriel hated Las Vegas; nevertheless, he agreed to spend the weekend there.

  Elia wanted to order the steak and lobster; instead, she ordered the tofu salad.

Use Semicolons to Join Items in a List When the Items Already Use Commas or Are Quite Long

On their trip the Singletons visited relatives in Nome, Alaska; Reno, Nevada; and Fresno, California.

My father showed up in a new black Honda Accord, which he could not possibly afford; handed the keys to my youngest daughter, who did not even know how to drive; and told her that the car was hers to keep.

Do Not Use a Semicolon to Join a Phrase, a Subordinate Clause, or a List to a Sentence

(incorrect)	*According to a recent poll; most Americans will never try drugs.*
(correct)	*According to a recent poll, most Americans will never try drugs.*
(incorrect)	*Sarah enjoyed the ski trip; although she did not like the cold weather.*
(correct)	*Sarah enjoyed the ski trip, although she did not like the cold weather.*
(incorrect)	*Tyler loved everything about high school baseball games; the crowds, the excitement, the food, even the uncomfortable bleachers.*
(correct)	*Tyler loved everything about high school baseball games: the crowds, the excitement, the food, even the uncomfortable bleachers.*

EXERCISE

Add or delete semicolons where necessary. (Some commas may need to be replaced with semicolons.)

1. Enrique wanted to study classical guitar Mary preferred to learn the clarinet.
2. As we walked around the block, we saw Mrs. O'Neil, the neighbor who hates our dogs, Cheryl Jackson, who teaches at the elementary school, and Elmer, who delivers our mail.
3. Because we were completely exhausted; we all went to bed and fell asleep.
4. The paint on his car had started to peel, therefore, Ron decided to have it repainted.
5. Last week it rained for four days; unfortunately, that amount of rain was not enough rain to end the drought.
6. Suzy loves the pastries from the local bakery; although she always feels ill after she eats them.
7. The play had finally ended, it was time to go home.

8. We have relatives living in Boulder, Colorado, Sioux Falls, South Dakota, and Henderson, Kentucky.

9. The Grinch hates many things about Christmas; the singing, the gift-giving, and especially the sense of joy and peace.

10. Tiger Woods practiced golf all day Saturday, then he played in a tournament on Sunday.

COLONS

Use a Colon after a Complete Main Clause to Introduce a List, Quotation, Summary, or Explanation

To use the colon correctly, make sure it follows *a complete main clause.*

- Introducing a List

  At the corner store, Seth always buys the same things: a bag of salted peanuts, a box of Cracker Jacks, and a large Diet Coke.

- Introducing a Quotation

  The speaker gave us one last look and then uttered his final bit of advice: "Always remember to floss."

- Introducing a Summary

  At the prom Dominic lost his wallet, spilled ketchup on his date's dress, and came down with the stomach flu: it was the worst night of his life.

- Introducing an Explanation

  His sister has a rather strange business: she sells ladybugs.

Do Not Use a Colon Unless It Follows a Complete Main Clause

(incorrect)	*Every Saturday night Bill watches reruns of: <u>Andy of Mayberry</u>, <u>Bonanza</u>, and <u>The Honeymooners</u>.*
(correct)	*Every Saturday night Bill watches reruns of <u>Andy of Mayberry</u>, <u>Bonanza</u>, and <u>The Honeymooners</u>.*
(incorrect)	*Ellie looked at Jethro's new car and said: "That's a mighty purty buggy you have there."*
(correct)	*Ellie looked at Jethro's new car and said, "That's a mighty purty buggy you have there."*

EXERCISE

Add or delete colons where necessary. (Other punctuation marks may need to be replaced with colons.)

1. It was time to perform the annual Christmas ritual; select a tree, cut it down, haul it home, set it up, and decorate it with ornaments.

2. Debbie's employer looked at her and said: "The customer is always right."

3. Last night's speaker has a strange hobby, he collects used horseshoes.

4. We are nearly out of bacon, eggs, bread, milk, and orange juice.

5. Mark Twain once made the following observation, "The lack of money is the root of all evil."

6. When it was finally time to leave: my mother burst into tears.

7. Jake could not believe it, his sister had won the state lottery.

8. Driving home from the Del Mar Fair, Steve thought of all the food he had eaten, hot apple pie, cinnamon rolls, frozen bananas dipped in chocolate, and huge swirls of cotton candy.

9. According to Oscar Wilde: "Marriage is hardly a thing that one can do now and again—except in America."

10. That textbook gives this bit of good advice: "Think in ink."

APOSTROPHES

Use Apostrophes to Form Contractions

The apostrophe replaces the omitted letter or letters in a contraction.

I am	=	*I'm*	*does not*	=	*doesn't*
is not	=	*isn't*	*did not*	=	*didn't*
are not	=	*aren't*	*were not*	=	*weren't*
cannot	=	*can't*	*will not*	=	*won't*
would not	=	*wouldn't*	*you are*	=	*you're*
it is	=	*it's*	*they are*	=	*they're*

Use Apostrophes to Form Possessives

- Add 's to make singular words possessive.

  the girl's hair   *nobody's business*
  Charles's car   *the dog's bed*
  his son-in-law's graduation   *someone's wallet*

- Add only an apostrophe to make possessives of plural words that already end in *s*.

  the three friends' conversation
  both teams' buses
  the Smiths' house
  my parents' car

- Add 's to make plural words that do not end in *s* possessive.

  the children's room
  the men's cars

- Add 's or only an apostrophe for certain expressions involving time or money.

  a dollar's worth of gas
  two dollars' worth
  a week's vacation
  two weeks' vacation

110

Do Not Use Apostrophes for Possessive Forms of Personal Pronouns

Incorrect	Correct
her's	*hers*
our's	*ours*
their's	*theirs*
it's (except for it is*)*	*its*
your's	*yours*

EXERCISE

Add apostrophes (or *'s*) where necessary.

1. That is Oscars football; he isnt using it today.
2. Do you think Louis slacks go well with his jacket?
3. The principals face turned beet red when he realized the car was ours.
4. For many people, two weeks vacation is not nearly long enough.
5. People thought that Carlas performance wasnt as powerful as Jerrys.
6. Its customary for the female praying mantis to eat her mate.
7. Were going to form a study group, and youre all invited to join.
8. The childrens toys and both of our bicycles were left out in the rain overnight.
9. The two brothers main concern was how to find a good therapist for their parents.
10. Two dollars worth of gas wont take people very far these days.

QUOTATION MARKS

Exact Words—Quotation Marks

Use quotation marks to enclose the exact words written or spoken by someone else.

As Oscar Wilde once said, "Fashion is a form of ugliness so intolerable that we have to alter it every six months."

Will Rogers stated, "Liberty doesn't work as well in practice as it does in speeches."

Paraphrases—No Quotation Marks

Do not use quotation marks when you paraphrase (reword) what someone else has spoken or written.

(exact words)	*Henry David Thoreau once wrote, "I should not talk so much about myself if there were anybody else whom I knew as well."*
(paraphrase)	*Henry David Thoreau once wrote that he would not talk about himself as much as he does if he knew anybody else as well as he knew himself.*

Transitions and Punctuation before Quotations

Introduce all quotations with transitions and appropriate punctuation.

- Use a comma when a transitional phrase introduces a quotation.

  According to a recent magazine article, "Apple computers have a very small but very significant share of the computer market."

- Use commas to set off an interrupting phrase that identifies a quotation.

  "The play is not yet over," said Mary, "but I want to leave anyway."

- Do not use a comma when a transitional phrase uses *that* before the quotation.

  Henry David Thoreau once wrote that "The light which puts out our eyes is darkness to us."

- Use a colon when a complete sentence introduces a quotation.

  The final sentence in Thoreau's Walden *provides a beautiful natural image: "The sun is but a morning star."*

- Do not use any punctuation to introduce a partial quotation.

  Shakespeare's King Lear described himself as "a man more sinned against that sinning."

Punctuation at the End of a Quotation

- Place periods and commas inside ending quotation marks.

  Randy turned to his brother and said, "Let's put up the Christmas lights."
  "It's time to leave for Las Vegas," said Bugsy.

- Place semicolons and colons outside ending quotation marks.

  Herman knew that some famous book started with "Call me Ishmael"; however, he couldn't remember which one.
  Michelle loves Seamus Heaney's poem "Digging": it reminds her of her childhood.

- Place question marks and exclamation points inside ending quotation marks if the quotation itself is a question or exclamation.

  "I think; therefore I am!" exclaimed Rene.
  Oedipus looked up and asked, "Exactly who is my mother?"
  Did George really say, "I cannot tell a lie"?

Long Quotations

If a quotation takes more than four lines to type, indent it ten lines from the left margin. Do not use quotation marks. Introduce the quotation with a complete sentence followed by a colon.

  One of my favorite passages is from Thoreau's Walden*:*

  > Why should we be in such desperate haste to succeed and in such desperate enterprises? If a man does not keep pace with his companions, perhaps it is because he hears a different drummer. Let him step to the music which he hears, however measured or far away. It is not important that he should mature as soon as an apple tree or an oak.

Quotations Within Quotations

Use single quotation marks when a quotation appears within another quotation.

> *According to the newspaper article, "A man walked into the crowded theater and yelled 'Fire!' just after the movie had started."*

EXERCISE

Add quotation marks where needed. When necessary, add the correct introductory punctuation marks, and place ending punctuation marks inside or outside the quotation marks as appropriate.

1. Ovid wrote To be loved, be lovable.
2. We are each our own devil, wrote Oscar Wilde, and we make this world our hell.
3. Who was it who said All's fair in love and war?
4. According to the seventeenth century French writer La Rouchefoucald We pardon to the extent that we love.
5. Darby also likes this quotation from La Rouchefoucald In jealousy there is more self-love than love.
6. An old English proverb states When poverty comes in at the door, love flies out the window.
7. In *Hamlet* Claudius tells Polonius that he doesn't think Hamlet is in love with Ophelia.
8. Rudyard Kipling must have been in a sour mood when he wrote the following It takes a great deal of Christianity to wipe out uncivilized Eastern instincts, such as falling in love at first sight.
9. Ah, love, wrote the poet, let us be true to one another.
10. Miss Piggy asked Kermit Do you love me

TITLES

Longer Works—Underline or Italicize

Underline or place in italics titles of longer works, such as books, magazines, plays, newspapers, CDs, and television programs.

- Books: <u>Moby Dick</u>, <u>Bartlett's Familiar Quotations</u>
- Plays: <u>The Glass Menagerie</u>, <u>A Doll House</u>
- Pamphlets: <u>Grooming Your Labrador</u>, <u>Charleston's Ten Best Restaurants</u>
- Long musical works: Mozart's <u>String Quartet in C Major</u>, Miles Davis's <u>Sketches of Spain</u>
- Long poems: <u>Howl</u>, <u>The Faerie Queene</u>
- Periodicals: <u>The Washington Post</u>, <u>Time</u>
- Films: <u>Titanic</u>, <u>Saving Private Ryan</u>
- Television and radio programs: <u>Sixty Minutes</u>, <u>Masterpiece Theater</u>
- Works of art: El Greco's <u>Saint Matthew</u>, <u>Nike of Samothrace</u>

Shorter Works—Use Quotation Marks

Use quotation marks to enclose titles of all shorter works, such as songs, poems, and short stories as well as parts of larger works, such as articles in magazines and chapters in books.

- Songs: "Wind beneath My Wings," "Friends"
- Poems: "My Last Duchess," "Dover Beach"
- Articles in periodicals: "Three-Headed Snake Born as Two-Headed Brother Looks On," "The Last Stand"
- Short stories: "A Jury of Her Peers," "Resurrection"
- Essays: "Male Fixations," "A Custody Fight for an Egg"
- Episodes of radio and television shows: "What's in a Name?"
- Subdivisions of books: "The Cassock" (Chapter 29 of <u>Moby Dick</u>)

Your Own Title—No Underlines, Italics, or Quotation Marks

Do not underline, italicize, or use quotation marks with the title of your own paper.

Exercise

Underline or use quotation marks with titles where necessary.

1. The movie Elizabeth contained many historical inaccuracies.
2. Ellen's favorite song was If I Loved You, played by Roland Kirk.
3. The article in Newsweek was entitled U.S. versus Microsoft: Slower Than the Web.
4. In Florence we saw the sculpture David, which was created by Michelangelo.
5. In Shakespeare's play The Merchant of Venice, there is much discussion of a "pound of flesh."
6. To begin the program, the orchestra played Johann Sebastian Bach's Brandenburg Concerto Number One.
7. Lilith is studying re-runs of the television program Frazier for her dissertation.
8. The novel Cold Mountain remained on bestseller lists longer than any book I can remember.
9. Professor Hibbard says that he teaches Robert Frost's poem Stopping by Woods on a Snowy Evening because of the special meter.
10. Susan loves to listen to Van Morrison's CD Tupelo Honey.

CAPITALIZATION

Capitalize

- The first letter of every sentence
- The pronoun *I*
- In titles, the first letter of the first and last words and of all other words except for *a, an,* or *the,* coordinating conjunctions (*and, but, or, nor, for, so, yet*), and prepositions (see page 78 for a list of prepositions).

  Dictionary of Philosophy and Religion
  "A Good Man Is Hard to Find"

- Names and titles of people: *President Clinton, William Shakespeare, Uncle Christopher, Ms. Hohman*
- Specific places: *Chicago, Smoky Mountains, Tennessee, The Armenian Cafe, Saturn, the South* (when referring to a place, not a direction)
- Ethnic, national or racial groups: *Native American, British, French, Canadian, Hispanic, Russian*
- Specific groups or organizations: *National Organization for Women, Girl Scouts of America, Methodists*
- Companies: *General Motors, Nordstrom, Pepsi Cola Bottling Company, R. J. Reynolds*
- Days of the week and months of the year: *Saturday, April*
- Holidays and historical events: *the Gulf War, Christmas, the Battle of Concord*
- Specific gods and religious writings: *God, Zeus, Buddha, Koran, Yahweh, Bible*

Do Not Capitalize

- General academic subjects: *psychology, math, history.* (But do capitalize specific class names—*Introduction to Psychology, Math 100*—as well as names of languages: *French, English, Spanish.*)
- Directions: *north, south, east, west.* (But do capitalize these words if they refer to specific places: *the South.*)
- Seasons: *spring, summer, winter, fall*

- General family names: *father, dad, mother, mom, sister, brother, uncle, aunt.* (But do capitalize such words when they are used as a person's name.)

  (no capitals)   *There is my brother standing next to my uncle.*

  (capitals)   *Tell Mom that Uncle George is here.*

- General titles of persons when not used as a name, such as *professor* or *doctor.* (But do capitalize such words when they are used as a name.)

  (no capitals)   *My professor is always late to class.*

  (capitals)   *I wish Professor Jones would arrive on time.*

- General nouns (also called common nouns): *car, dog, student, house, college*

Exercise

Correct any errors in capitalization.

1. Flo saw aunt beatrice on new year's day.
2. When alvin visits the southwest, he always goes to santa fe.
3. The film about islamic history was produced by warner brothers.
4. On friday a yugoslavian immigrant will explain about the cars.
5. As carl's professor was lecturing on <u>paradise lost</u>, carl was thinking about christmas.
6. One must go south from los angeles to reach san diego.
7. When i buy cookies from the girl scouts, i tend to overspend.
8. In yellowstone national park we camped near some people from russia.
9. When my father thinks of the new york stock exchange, he worries about bears.
10. Every spring my aunt griselda's attention turns to geoffrey chaucer, who wrote <u>the canterbury tales</u>.

NUMBERS

Spell These

- Numbers that require only one or two words

  one, twenty-three, ten million

- Numbers at the beginning of a sentence

  Two hundred thirty-five miles is a long distance to roller blade.

Use Numerals for These

- Dates

  June 24, 1981   55 B.C.

- Addresses

  3245 Sisyphus Street
  Stonewall, Nebraska 90345

- Numbers of three or more words

  2,115   110

- Decimals, percentages, and fractions

  7.5   75% (75 percent is also acceptable), 1/8

- Sections of books or plays

  Chapter 26, page 390   Act 5, scene 2, lines 78–90

- Exact amounts of money (round dollar or cent amounts may be spelled)

  $10.86 $6,723,001
  $10.00 or ten dollars (but not 10 dollars)

- Scores and statistics

  Padres 10 Reds 0   a ratio of 4 to 1

- Time of day (but spell the number when *o'clock* is used)

  5:23   12:45   ten o'clock (but not 10 o'clock)

- Numbers in a list may also be spelled, providing *all* of them are spelled

We bought 100 paper plates, 30 packs of napkins, and 115 plastic spoons.

or

We bought one hundred paper plates, thirty packs of napkins, and one hundred fifteen plastic spoons.

EXERCISE

Correct any errors in the use of numbers.

1. 313 Minnesotans watched the Whippets beat the Troglodytes fifteen to fourteen.
2. On June first the 4 members of my family moved to sixty-nine Beelzebub Street, Mephistopheles, New Jersey.
3. By five thirty-two I had won two dollars and sixty cents at the racetrack.
4. When 5,000 people lined up to buy 300 tickets, the promoters were puzzled.
5. The nurses were bargaining for a five percent raise, but they were offered only two point five percent.
6. The membership of the assembly is as follows: one hundred five Republicans, 50 Democrats, thirty-four Independents, and 2 Mugwumps.
7. By the end of Act Five of <u>Hamlet</u>, 7 people have died.
8. When Chris saw that the Chargers had lost twenty-four to twenty, she despaired.
9. At ten forty-five Professor Hohman told us to reconsider the meaning of Chapter Forty-three of <u>Tristram Shandy</u>.
10. Michelle had four hundred twelve photographs taken before she found 1 that she liked.

COMMONLY CONFUSED WORDS

The following words are commonly confused because they sound alike, look alike, or have similar meanings. Use this list to learn those that give you trouble.

a
: Used before words that begin with consonant sounds.
  a porcupine, a bat, a sword, a good boy

an
: Used before words that begin with vowel sounds.
  an apple, an honor, an unusual cloud formation

and
: Joins words, phrases, or clauses.
  John and Abigail

---

accept
: To take or receive what is offered or given.
  Lawrence accepted his punishment.

except
: Excluding.
  Candy was on everyone's desk except mine.

---

advice
: An opinion about what to do. A noun.
  The coach gave Brutus advice about how to make the team.

advise
: To give advice. A verb.
  Rene's employer advised her to control her temper.

---

affect
: To influence or to produce a change in. Usually a verb.
  His bad attitude affects his entire family.

effect
: A result. Usually a noun.
  Howard's announcement did not have the effect he had hoped for.

---

all ready
: Completely ready.
  After dinner we were all ready to take a nap.

already
: By or before a certain time.
  Has he already left?

---

all right	Satisfactory or unhurt. *After the accident Jill said that she felt all right.*
alright	A misspelling. Do not use it.
among	Use with three or more things or ideas. *Mr. Griswold slowly walked among the worried applicants.*
between	Use with two things or ideas. *Jenna could not decide between Gambit and Wolverine.*
amount	Use with uncountable quantities, such as milk, oil, salt, or flour. *The amount of sugar the recipe calls for is two cups.*
number	Use with countable quantities. *The number of people in the room exceeded fire regulations.*
anxious	Apprehensive, uneasy, worried. *The sailor was anxious about the approaching storm.*
eager	Looking forward to, enthusiastic. *Isaac was eager to try out his new pair of skis.*
complement	That which completes or brings to perfection. *Your alligator shoes complement your mink coat.*
compliment	An expression of praise, respect, or courtesy. *Mr. Salas received many compliments for his Christmas decorations.*
conscience	Knowledge or sense of right and wrong. *Joey's conscience helped him to make the right decision.*
conscious	Aware or awake. *Frank was conscious of all the stares and snickers.*

farther	Describes physical distance.
	He walked farther than I did.
further	Describes nonphysical distance.
	I have gone further in my studies than he has.

fewer	Use with items that can be counted.
	Fewer people attended this year's lecture than last year's.
less	Use with amounts not usually counted, such as water or air.
	There was less sand on the beach after the storm.

lay	To put something down.
	Lay the paper on the table.
	Other forms: laying, laid
	He is laying the paper on the table.
	He laid the paper on the table.
	He has laid the paper on the table.
lie	To rest or recline.
	The toys lie all over the yard.
	Other forms: lying, lay, lain
	The toys are lying all over the yard right now.
	The toys lay all over the yard yesterday.
	The toys have lain all over the yard for three days.

lead	A heavy metal or a part of a pencil.
	Alchemists believe they can turn lead into gold.
	Present tense of the verb *to lead.*
	Every year Mr. Powell leads the Easter parade.
led	Past tense of the verb *to lead.*
	Karen led her friends to the hidden waterfall.

lend	To give to someone temporarily. A verb. *Judy will lend you the money.*
loan	Something given to someone temporarily. A noun. *Judy gave me a loan of $10,000.*
loose	Not confined or restrained, not tight. *The hamster was loose and running through the house.*
lose	To misplace, to be defeated. *Lester did not believe he would lose the race.*
passed	Form of *to pass*. To go or move forward, through, or out. *As I drove home, I passed a grocery store.*
past	Gone by, ended, over; the time that has gone by; beyond. *His past mistakes have caught up with him.* *In the past, I have always tried to be fair.* *Jack waved as he drove past Jill's house.*
personal	Private or individual. *One should not conduct personal business on company time.*
personnel	Persons employed. *All personnel must submit their time sheets on Friday.*
precede	To go before. *Thanksgiving precedes Christmas.*
proceed	To advance or go on. *After lunch Ms. Johnstone proceeded with her report.*
principal	The head of a school; also, first in rank or importance. *The principal of the school called a morning assembly.* *Our principal concern is the safety of the children.*
principle	A fundamental truth, law, or doctrine. *One should always act upon principle.*

quit	To stop doing something.	*Henry quit drinking coffee last week.*
quite	Completely or really.	*It was quite cool last January.*
quiet	Silent.	*The quiet evening soon darkened into night.*

than	A comparison.	*My brother is stronger than your brother.*
then	At that time, soon afterwards, next.	*I ate fifty cherries, and then I began to feel sick.*

their	Belonging to them.	*The team members congratulated their coach.*
there	In that place.	*Let's park the car over there.*
they're	They are.	*"They're back," said the little girl ominously.*

to	In the direction of.	*We went to Blockbuster last night.*
	Verb form.	*We are ready to eat.*
too	Also; more than enough.	*Jackson decided that he wanted an apple pie too.*
		Too many people were standing on the tiny stage.
two	The number after one.	*His two sons were arrested last night.*

weather	Climate; atmospheric conditions.	*The rainy weather is beginning to bother him.*
whether	Suggests alternatives; similar to *if*. Does not require "or not."	*He did not know whether to stay or go.*

we're	We are.
	We're almost there.
were	Past tense form of *to be.*
	We were late for dessert.
where	Indicates place.
	Where did I put my glasses?

your	Belonging to you.
	Give me all of your money.
you're	You are.
	You're not really serious, are you?

Exercise

Correct any errors in word choice.

1. Marlyle said it was alright with her if I did not follow her advise.
2. As we drove to Disneyland, my anxious daughters kept asking me how much further it was.
3. Sara was to excited to fall asleep when she laid down for her nap.
4. Less people attended the concert this year then last year.
5. When he heard Johnny's excuse, the principle did not know weather to laugh or cry.
6. Did his lecture have any effect upon your conscience at all?
7. A green pickup sped passed the school and slammed into the back of you're car.
8. Mr. and Mrs. Twohey would not except there son's collect phone call.
9. Thunderball lead the entire race until just before the finish line, were he lost by a nose.
10. Just between the three of us, do you think we will loose this election?

Spelling

Buy and Use a Dictionary

Small, inexpensive paperback dictionaries are available in nearly every bookstore or supermarket. Keep one next to you as you write and get used to using it.

Pay Attention to Your Own Reactions As You Write

If you are not confident of the spelling of a word, assume you have probably misspelled it and use your dictionary to check it.

Don't Rely Too Much on Spelling Checkers

Although spelling checkers are excellent tools that you should use, don't assume they will solve all of your spelling problems because they won't.

Use Memory Tricks

You can memorize the spelling of many words by using some memory techniques.

There is a rat in separate.

The first ll's are parallel in parallel.

Dessert has two ss's because everyone wants two desserts.

Read More Often

The most effective way to become a better speller (and, for that matter, a better writer and thinker) is to read on a regular basis. If you do not read novels, perhaps now is the time to start.

Learn the Basic Rules of Spelling

The following explanations should help you improve your spelling. However, note that each of these "rules" contains numerous exceptions. You must use a dictionary if you have any doubt about the spelling of a word.

❖ *I Before E*

Use *i* before *e*
Except after *c*
Or when sounded like *ay*
As in *neighbor* or *weigh*.

IE	EI (after C)	EI (sounded like Ay)
grief	*deceive*	*sleigh*
niece	*ceiling*	*eight*
belief	*receipt*	*weigh*
achieve	*perceive*	*neighbor*

Some exceptions (there are many): *ancient, caffeine, height, their, society, either*

❖ Adding Letters to Words Ending in -*y*

Change the *y* to *i* when the *y* follows a consonant.

deny → *denies*
hobby → *hobbies*

Do not change the *y* to *i* if the *y* follows a vowel.

delay → *delays*
key → *keys*

Do not change the *y* to *i* when adding -*ing* to a verb.

say → *saying*
study → *studying*

❖ Keeping or Dropping a Silent Final -*e*

In general, drop the final -*e* before an ending beginning with a vowel.

move + ing = moving
advise + able = advisable

In general, keep the final -*e* before an ending beginning with a consonant.

hope + less = hopeless
safe + ly = safely

There are many exceptions to both these general rules.

courage + ous = courageous

judge + ment = judgment

❖ Doubling the Final Consonant

When adding letters to a word, double the final consonant if there is only one vowel in front of the consonant.

one vowel (double)	two vowels (no double)
drop + ing = dropping	*sleep + ing = sleeping*
slap + ed = slapped	*clean + ed = cleaned*

Apply this rule to multi-syllable words only if the last syllable is stressed.

last syllable stressed	last syllable not stressed
expel + ing = expelling	*answer + ing = answering*
occur + ed = occurred	*happen + ed = happened*

❖ Using Prefixes

A prefix is one or more letters added at the start of a word to change its meaning. Do not change any letters of the base word when you add a prefix to it.

prefix + base = new word

im + possible = impossible

mis + spell = misspell

il + legal = illegal

un + necessary = unnecessary

EXERCISE

Correct any errors in spelling.

1. Janet could hardly beleive that she had mispelled such an easy word.
2. Eight tiny reindeer pulled the sliegh high over the tops of the chimnies.
3. Bald eagles are rarly seen in these mountains, and it is ilegal to hunt them.

4. Too many innaccuracies in spelling can iritate any reader.

5. When he admitted how many chocolates he had eaten, everyone gaspped.

6. Alicia was begining to understand that something was diffrent about this town.

7. The two attornies decided to falsify the missing reciept.

8. When he said he was quiting, everyone in the audeince was surprised.

9. In the excitment of the party, no one noticed that a theft had occured.

10. Herman was controling the model plane while his father gave him encouragment.

PART 4

ESL CONCERNS

USING *A*, *AN*, OR *THE*

USING HELPING VERBS AND MAIN VERBS

PLACING ADJECTIVES CORRECTLY AND USING PARTICIPLES AS ADJECTIVES

Using *A*, *An*, or *The*

Singular Count Nouns

Count nouns refer to nouns that you can count: one city, two cities; one person, two persons.

- If a singular count noun is general or is being introduced for the first time, use *a* or *an*.

*Yesterday I saw **a car** with two teenagers in it.*   (first introduced, general)

***A motorcycle** started to follow it.*   (first introduced, general)

- If a singular count noun is specifically identified or has been introduced earlier, use *the*.

***The car** was traveling east on Highway 78.*   (introduced earlier)

*Soon **the motorcycle following it** pulled off the road.*   (introduced earlier, specific)

- If a singular count noun is specifically identified when it is first introduced, use *the* with it.

***The car that hit me** did not stop.*   (specifically identified)

Plural Count Nouns

If the meaning of a plural count noun is specific, use *the*. Do not use *the* if its meaning is general. (Never use *a* or *an* with plural count nouns.)

*Loud noises cause **the windows** in my house to rattle.*   (specific)

*Loud noises can cause **windows** to rattle.*   (general)

Noncount Nouns

Noncount nouns do not have plural forms, so they are considered uncountable. Here are some common noncount nouns:

Food and drink:	*meat, bacon, spinach, celery, rice, flour, butter, water, milk, wine, lemonade*
Nonfood material:	*equipment, furniture, luggage, rain, silver, gasoline, leather*
Abstractions:	*anger, beauty, happiness, honesty, courage*

Do not use *a* or *an* with a noncount noun. If its meaning is specific, use *the*. Do not use *the* if its meaning is general.

Honesty is the best policy.   (general)

*I admire **the courage that you showed by your actions.***   (specific)

Proper Nouns

- Use *the* with plural proper nouns (*the United States, the Smiths*).
- Do not use *the* with most singular proper nouns (*John, San Diego, Germany*). There are, however, many exceptions. Use *the* with singular proper nouns when they are names of oceans, seas, and rivers (*the Mississippi River, the Atlantic Ocean*), names using *of* (*the Republic of China, the University of Colorado*), and names of large regions, deserts, and peninsulas (*the Mideast, the Sahara Desert, the Iberian Peninsula*).

EXERCISE

Use *a, an,* or *the* where necessary.

1. Jerry owns big black cat and tiny toy poodle.
2. I gave my money to man who organized New Year's Day parade.
3. Principal led angry people into his office.
4. When she was robbed for third time, Dora decided to buy security system.
5. Person who owns red Honda is shouting at me.
6. My daughter was excited when she saw Christmas presents that Santa had brought.
7. Whenever we go to baseball game, my son buys hot dog.
8. His decision to tell truth required courage and honesty.
9. Last year I visited Philippines for first time.
10. When he makes more money, Horace will buy new car to replace Pontiac GrandAm he has now.

USING HELPING VERBS AND MAIN VERBS

Choosing the right combination of helping verbs and main verbs can be difficult if English is your second language. To make the correct choices, you must first understand a few things about main verbs and helping verbs.

- If the verb consists of one word, it is a main verb (MV).

    MV
    *The old waiter **stared** at the table.*

- If the verb consists of two or more words, the last word of the verb is the main verb (MV). The earlier words are helping verbs (HV).

    HV MV
    *The old waiter **is staring** at the table.*

    HV MV
    *The old waiter **must leave** soon.*

Helping Verbs

There are only twenty-three helping verbs in English, so it is not difficult to become familiar with them. Nine of the helping verbs are called *modals*. They are always helping verbs. The other fourteen words sometimes function as helping verbs and sometimes as main verbs. Here are the twenty-three helping verbs:

Modals:	*can*	*will*	*shall*	*may*
	could	*would*	*should*	*might*
				must

Forms of *do:*	*do, does, did*
Forms of *have:*	*have, has, had*
Forms of *be:*	*am, is, are, was, were, be, being, been*

Main Verbs

To use helping verbs and main verbs correctly, you need to know the forms that main verbs can take. All main verbs use five forms (except for *be,* which uses eight).

Base Form	-S Form	Past Tense	Past Participle	Present Participle
walk	walks	walked	walked	walking
call	calls	called	called	calling
eat	eats	ate	eaten	eating
give	gives	gave	given	giving
ring	rings	rang	rung	ringing

Notice that the past tense and the past participle of *call* and *walk* are spelled the same way, by adding -*ed*. They are called regular verbs. However, the past tense and past participle of *eat* and *ring* change spelling dramatically. These are irregular verbs. If you are unsure how to spell any form of a verb, use your dictionary. The spelling of each form is listed there.

Combining Helping Verbs and Main Verbs

When combining helping verbs and main verbs, pay careful attention to the verb forms that you use.

- **Modal + base form.** After one of the nine modals (*can, could, will, would, shall, should, may, might, must*), use the base form of a verb.

  (incorrect) He *will leaving* soon.

  (correct) He *will leave* soon.

- **Do, does, did + base form.** When forms of *do* are used as helping verbs, use the base form after them.

  (incorrect) *Did your daughter asked you for a present?*

  (correct) *Did your daughter ask you for a present?*

- **Have, has, or had + past participle.** Use the past participle form after *have, has,* or *had*. Check a dictionary if you are not sure how to spell the past participle.

  (incorrect) *The monkey has eating all of the fruit.*

  (correct) *The monkey has eaten all of the fruit.*

  (incorrect) *We had walk ten miles before noon.*

  (correct) *We had walked ten miles before noon.*

- **Forms of be + present participle.** To show continuous action, use the present participle (the -*ing* form) after a form of *be* (*am, is, are, was, were, be, been*).

(incorrect)	*I reading the book.*
(correct)	*I am reading the book.*

- **Forms of be + past participle.** To express passive voice (the subject receives the action rather than performs it), use a form of *be* followed by the past participle form.

(incorrect)	*The football was threw by the quarterback.*
(correct)	*The football was thrown by the quarterback.*

EXERCISE

Correct any errors when helping verbs and main verbs do not match.

1. After breakfast, my uncle will reading the paper.
2. He did not gave me any help with my test.
3. The man who was standing at the corner has taking that woman's purse.
4. All of the food at the banquet was ate before it was time to leave.
5. Did your son walked all the way home?
6. Maureen insists that she does not wants any help.
7. Everyone who meets that man is frighten by his violent behavior.
8. A man has jump off the bridge.
9. Please be quiet because I am concentrate on my homework.
10. If you want dessert, you must eating all your dinner.

PLACING ADJECTIVES CORRECTLY AND USING PARTICIPLES AS ADJECTIVES

Place Adjectives Carefully

Adjectives usually precede the nouns that they modify. When one or more adjectives precede a noun, follow these general guidelines. (These guidelines are not iron-clad "rules," so don't be surprised when you encounter exceptions.)

❖ **General Order of Adjectives**

- Articles and noun markers, possessives, quantity words, numerals

  a, an, the, this, that, his, Jim's, many, some, two, six

- Evaluative words

  beautiful, interesting, courageous, determined

- Size

  large, small, gigantic

- Shape

  round, square, short, long

- Age

  young, old, new

- Color

  blue, red

- Nationality

  American, Chinese, European

- Religious Faith

  Buddhist, Catholic, Protestant

- Material

  leather, vinyl, wooden

- Noun used as adjective

  basketball (as in *basketball* game)

trash (as in *trash* can)

In general, avoid long strings of adjectives. More than two or three adjectives in a row is too many.

Use the Present Participle and the Past Participle as Adjectives with Care

• The present participle is the *-ing* form of a verb (*eating, sleeping*). Words modified by it are *causing* or *producing* an effect. For example, in the following sentence, the movie is causing or producing the depressing feeling.

The <u>depressing</u> movie ruined my entire evening.

(not *the depressed movie*)

• The past participle usually ends in *-ed, -d, -en, n,* or *-t.* Words modified by it are *undergoing* an experience, not causing one. In the following sentence, for instance, the sales clerk is undergoing the depressed feeling, not causing it.

The <u>depressed</u> sales clerk stared at his meager paycheck.

(not *the depressing sales clerk*)

EXERCISE

Correct any errors in the placement of adjectives or in the use present and past participles as adjectives.

1. A blue ugly car drove down the deserting street.
2. I was disgusting by the wool smelly sweater.
3. Al picked up two square tiny dice and threw them across the table.
4. The ancient manuscripts were fascinated to the two archeologists.
5. After the grueling basketball game, Jackson was completely exhausting.
6. It was surprising to see a small adobe hut in the middle of the city.
7. We decided to have dinner at a Chinese expensive restaurant.
8. Marianne wore a gold stunning ornate bracelet to last night's concert.
9. The two silver roses were an unexpected gift from my sister.
10. The movie was so bored that we left halfway through.

WRITING WITH STYLE

NOT TOO FORMAL—NOT TOO INFORMAL

AVOIDING CLICHÉS AND EUPHEMISMS

CUTTING EXCESS WORDS

USING PARALLEL SENTENCE STRUCTURE

VARYING SENTENCE LENGTH AND STRUCTURE

NOT TOO FORMAL—NOT TOO INFORMAL

Think of college writing as semi-formal writing. Your papers should not sound like the confusing mumbo-jumbo that you find in legal contracts. But neither should they sound like the informal slang of someone who hasn't quite grown up yet.

Overly Formal Language and Jargon

Don't try to impress your readers with fancy words. Overly formal words and phrases make your writing sound pretentious, not profound. Jargon, which is specialized language used by technical or professional groups, will have the same effect. Don't use it when you are writing college papers for a general audience.

Don't misunderstand. You should always try to improve your vocabulary. But don't let your words draw too much attention to themselves. Here are some examples of overly formal expressions and jargon, along with their plain-language equivalents:

Overdone	Plain language
family residence	home
verbally communicate	talk
commence	begin
become cognizant of	realize
prognosticate	predict
utilization	use
maternal parent	mother
monetary outlay	expense
facilitate	help
optimal	best

(overly formal)   *When my maternal parent commenced to verbally communicate her emotional ire to me, I became cognizant of the fact that I should leave the family residence.*

(plain language)   *When my mother told me how angry she was, I realized that I had better leave the house.*

Informal Language and Slang

Writing that is too informal can be as distracting as pretentious, formal writing. And slang, the informal expressions that belong to particular groups, is almost never appropriate in college papers. Replace such words and expressions with a plain-language equivalent.

Too Informal	Plain Language
a lot, lots of, a bunch	many, several
kind of, sort of	rather, somewhat
ripped off	stolen, cheated
loaded	intoxicated, drugged
gross	disgusting
laid-back	relaxed
uptight	nervous, tense
no brainer	easy
hang out	spend some time with (or at)

(too informal) *Lots of us were sweating the next test, but then our teacher said it would be a real no brainer.*

(plain language) *Many of us were worried about the next test, but then our teacher said that it would not be a difficult one.*

EXERCISE

Rewrite the following sentences so that they are neither too formal nor too informal.

1. I was floored when I heard what he had said.

2. An awful lot of people think he's got a serious attitude problem.

3. To relieve himself of excess weight, he started to attend his local gymnastics facility.

4. After commencing bowling, I became cognizant of my sore thumb.

5. George's maternal parent started to bawl at the funeral.

6. Deciding where to go for vacation was a real no brainer.

7. Although I love the beach, I know that excessive solar exposure can damage my skin.

8. It blew my mind when Janice said she would hang out with me.

9. Alger opened his lunch box and stared at the sustenance within it.

10. He is a very laid back guy, so being ripped off by that clerk did not bother him.

Avoiding Clichés and Euphemisms

Clichés

Clichés are overused phrases or expressions that have lost their freshness and originality. They make your writing sound superficial and unoriginal, so you should either eliminate them from your paper altogether or replace them with fresh, descriptive expressions of your own.

The problem is learning to recognize clichés when you see them. If you don't know that an expression is a cliché, you won't be able to replace it. One way to spot them is to know that clichés are predictable. If you say only the first few words of a cliché, the reader can predict exactly what will follow.

Because they are clichés, it is easy to complete the following the expressions:

last but not	*least*
in this day and	*age*
better late than	*never*
easier said than	*done*
blind as	*a bat*
quiet as	*a mouse*
sly as	*a fox*
avoid like	*the plague*
slept like	*a log*
by leaps and	*bounds*
raining cats and	*dogs*
between a rock and	*a hard place*
no use crying over	*spilt milk*
up a creek without	*a paddle*
off the beaten	*track*
selling like	*hotcakes*
it goes without	*saying*
it's a crying	*shame*
that's the last	*straw*
shake like a	*leaf*
the crack of	*dawn*

as high as a	*kite*
take it for	*granted*
it's a dog-eat-	*dog world*
add insult to	*injury*

Euphemisms

Euphemisms are expressions used in place of words that seem harsh, insensitive, or offensive. We use *passed away* to refer to death, *senior citizens* to refer to old people, and *going to the bathroom* to refer to urinating or defecating. Euphemisms are an important part of our language, especially when you are trying to be polite or tactful. But euphemisms can also be wordy and indirect as well as evasive and dishonest.

Euphemism	*Plain Language*
adult entertainment	pornography
preowned automobile	used car
economically deprived	poor
strategic withdrawal	retreat
revenue enhancements	taxes
staff reductions	layoffs, firings
correctional facilities	prisons
negative cash flow	losing money
stretching the truth	lying

Correcting Clichés and Euphemisms

Replace the cliché or euphemism with plain language that expresses what you want to say.

(weak)   *The magazine said that preowned Hondas were the cream of the crop, but I couldn't buy one because of my negative cash flow.*

(better)   *The magazine said that used Hondas were the best on the market, but I couldn't buy one because I was already spending more money than I was making.*

(weak)   *Last but not least, parents in this day and age need to teach their children why they should avoid adult entertainment like the plague.*

(better)   *Finally, parents today need to teach their children why they should refuse to read, view, or buy any kind of pornography.*

EXERCISE

Rewrite the following sentences to replace clichés and euphemisms.

1. After the exhausting game, Carlton slept like a log.
2. It was raining cats and dogs on the trip home from San Francisco.
3. Our family budget is experiencing a negative cash flow, but saving money is easier said than done.
4. The Internet has hundreds of sites devoted solely to adult entertainment.
5. After our business went bankrupt, I felt as if we were up a creek without a paddle.
6. Lyle was shaking like a leaf as he walked out onto the stage.
7. Because she did not want to disturb her parents, Jenna was as quiet as a mouse when she came home at the crack of dawn.
8. Carl had to spend a night in our local correctional facility when he was arrested for driving under the influence of alcohol.
9. The salesperson at the car lot thought he was being as sly as a fox, but I could read him like a book.
10. Last but not least, we should never stretch the truth.

CUTTING EXCESS WORDS

Don't worry about wordiness as you write the first draft of your paper. Instead, work on developing and organizing your ideas. Once that first draft is complete, however, start cutting excess words and rewording needlessly roundabout sentences

Redundancies

Redundant wording repeats an idea using different words, so often it is not easy to spot. Whenever possible, eliminate redundant wording.

(redundant)	*We left for Rome at 10:00 **a.m. in the morning.***
(concise)	*We left for Rome at 10:00 a.m.*
(redundant)	***Whenever it rains, we always** stay indoors.*
(concise)	*Whenever it rains, we stay indoors.*
(redundant)	*My **father is a man** who always keeps his word.*
(concise)	*My father always keeps his word.*
(redundant)	*My new coat was very **expensive in price.***
(concise)	*My new coat was very expensive.*
(redundant)	*Good baseball players know the **basic fundamentals** of the game.*
(concise)	*Good baseball players know the fundamentals of the game.*

Needless Repetition

Needless repetition of a word or phrase also weakens sentences. (Some repetition, however, can be effective when used for emphasis.)

(repetitive)	*My favorite **picture** is the **picture** of our house in Newport Beach.*
(concise)	*My favorite picture is the one of our house in Newport Beach.*

(repetitive)	*When my sister called me on the **telephone** at **two o'clock this morning**, I told her that **two o'clock in the morning** was too early **in the morning** for her to call on **the telephone**.*
(concise)	*When my sister phoned me at two o'clock this morning, I told her that she should not be calling so early.*
(repetitive)	*The death **penalty** is an unfair **penalty** that is applied more often to **poor people** because **poor people** do not have the money to hire expensive attorneys.*
(concise)	*The death penalty is unfair because it is applied more often to poor people, who cannot afford to hire attorneys.*
(repetitive)	*The **light** from his flashlight nearly blinded me when he shined the **light** directly into my eyes.*
(concise)	*His flashlight nearly blinded me when he shined it directly into my eyes.*

Roundabout Phrases

Replace phrases that say in four or five words what can be said in one or two.

Roundabout	Concise
at all times	always
at the present time	now
at this point in time	now
on many occasions	often
in this modern day and age	today
because of the fact that	because
due to the fact that	because
for the purpose of	for
until such time as	until
in spite of the fact that	although, even though
make reference to	refer to
be of the opinion that	think, believe
in the event that	if

To Be Verbs, *There are, It is*

- Replace *to be* verbs (*am, are, is, was, were, been, being, be*) with action verbs to make your writing more concise.

(wordy)   *He **is** the one who stole the tickets.*

(concise)   *He **stole** the tickets.*

(wordy)   *My suggestion **is** that we leave by 10:00.*

(concise)   *I **suggest** that we leave by 10:00.*

(wordy)   *That movie **is** a portrayal of the violence of inner city gang life.*

(concise)   *That movie **portrays** the violence of inner city gang life.*

(wordy)   *Ernest and Oscar **were** the recipients of a $10,000 inheritance.*

(concise)   *Ernest and Oscar **inherited** $10,000.*

- Sentences beginning with *It* and *There* often contain needless words.

(wordy)   *There were three people waiting to talk to the Pope.*

(improved)   *Three people were waiting to talk to the Pope.*

(wordy)   *It is imperative that we lower the rate of crime in our city.*

(improved)   *We must lower the rate of crime in our city.*

(wordy)   *There is a belief held by many people that our social security system needs to be improved.*

(improved)   *Many people believe that our social security system needs to be improved.*

EXERCISE

Revise the following sentences to eliminate unnecessary wordiness.

1. In my memory I remember what my childhood house where I grew up looked like.
2. The student who attended the orientation was attending it because it was a mandatory orientation.
3. He left the room because of the fact that the television was too loud in volume.

4. There are three people who are going to the baseball game.

5. It is my father's desire that we drive to Utah this summer.

6. Arnold was very eager to discuss the basic fundamentals of gymnastics.

7. We will remain seated in our chairs until such time as the show ends.

8. The desk that I want to buy is that desk in the corner.

9. In this modern day and age, no one should ever go hungry or need more food.

10. My brother was the winner of the lottery in spite of the fact that he is a convicted felon.

USING PARALLEL SENTENCE STRUCTURE

Parallelism refers to wording ideas similarly if they are joined with a coordinating conjunction (such as *and* or *or*), if they are combined in a list, or if they are combined with correlative conjunctions.

Ideas Joined by *and* or *or*

Two ideas joined by *and* or *or* should be worded similarly. Notice the differences in the following examples:

(not parallel)   *My favorite sports are **swimming** and **to jog**.*

(parallel)   *My favorite sports are **swimming** and **jogging**.*

(not parallel)   *To do well in life, you need to **set goals** and **risks should be taken**.*

(parallel)   *To do well in life, you need to **set goals** and **take risks**.*

Items in a List

When you write three or more ideas in a list, you should word them similarly, just as you do when you join two ideas with a coordinating conjunction.

(non-parallel words)   *The town was full of **bribers, people who cheat, chiselers**, and **some were swindlers**.*

(parallel words)   *The town was full of **bribers, cheaters, chiselers**, and **swindlers**.*

(non-parallel phrases)   *He spent most of his free time **strolling on the beach**, **he visited local museums**, and **talking to the local shop owners**.*

(parallel phrases)   *He spent most of his free time **strolling on the beach**, **visiting local museums**, and **talking to the local shop owners**.*

Items Joined by Correlative Conjunctions

The most common correlative conjunctions are *either . . . or; neither . . . nor; not only . . . but also; both . . . and.* Follow the principles of parallel sentence structure when you use these correlatives.

(not parallel)	*The timber wolf will **either** <u>adapt to its new environment</u> **or** <u>it will die a slow death</u>.* (verb phrase combined with main clause)
(parallel)	*The timber wolf will **either** <u>adapt to its new environment</u> **or** <u>die a slow death</u>.* (verb phrase combined with verb phrase)
(parallel)	***Either** <u>the timber wolf will adapt to its new environment</u> **or** <u>it will die a slow death</u>.* (main clause combined with main clause)

EXERCISE

Revise the following sentences to correct any errors in parallelism.

1. Before we leave, we need to fill the car with gas and some food must be bought.
2. In the deserted garage we found an old lawnmower, a rake was there, and two shovels.
3. The skier stepped into his ski bindings, grabbed his poles, and then he had fallen flat on his face.
4. His father told him either to cut his hair or he had to stay home.
5. Too much exposure to the sun can cause mild sunburn today and in the future you might get serious skin cancer.
6. As he walked down the street, children laughed at him, and stones were thrown at him by grown men.
7. Last summer we visited relatives in Sioux Falls, gambling was done in Deadwood City, and we water-skied on Lake Ponset.
8. The rainy weather makes me feel not only depressed but also causes my knees to ache.
9. The cabin disappointed Sergio because the windows were broken and it had shabby furniture.
10. Esmerelda's job consisted of approving all work orders, addressing the invoices, and the files were to be organized by her.

VARYING SENTENCE LENGTH AND STRUCTURE

Sentences that are all the same length or that all follow the same pattern can be very boring to read. To prevent your reader from nodding off in the middle of your paper, try writing sentences that differ from each other in length and structure.

Combine Short Sentences

One of the chief causes of monotonous writing is a series of brief sentences, one after the other.

> *My backyard is turning into a real mess. I hate to do yard work. I haven't mown my lawn for three weeks. I also haven't weeded the garden. I should mow the lawn today. I think I'll watch a movie instead. My neighbor has a beautiful backyard. He loves to do yard work.*

You can combine short sentences several ways.

- Use a comma and a coordinating conjunction between them.
  The seven coordinating conjunctions are *and, but, or, nor, for, so, yet.*
  I should mow the lawn today, **but** *I think I'll watch a movie instead.*

- Use a semicolon between them.
  I haven't mown my lawn for three weeks; I also haven't weeded the garden.

- Use a semicolon and a transition expression between them.

  Here are some common transition expressions:

accordingly	hence	next	thus
also	however	nonetheless	on the other hand
besides	instead	otherwise	as a result
consequently	meanwhile	similarly	for example
finally	moreover	still	for instance
further	namely	then	in addition
furthermore	nevertheless	therefore	in fact

*I should mow the lawn today; **however,** I think I'll watch a movie instead.*

Note: Use a semicolon, not a comma, to join two sentences with a transition.

- Use subordinate clauses.

  Change some of the short sentences to subordinate clauses. Then join them to the remaining sentences. (Subordinate clauses cannot stand alone.) The following subordinators will change a main clause to a subordinate clause.

after	so that	that	who(ever)
although	than	which	whom(ever)
as	though	whose	
as if	unless		
as long as	until		
because	when		
before	whenever		
even though	where		
if	wherever		
since	while		

*My backyard is turning into a real mess **because** I hate to do yard work.*
*My neighbor, **who** loves to do yard work, has a beautiful backyard.*

Use Sentence Openers

Too many short, choppy sentences can be distracting, but a more common cause of lifeless writing is a repetitive sentence structure. The most commonly repeated sentence structure—and the easiest to vary—opens with the subject and verb of its main clause. Here are some examples of this common sentence pattern.

      S   V
Television has been blamed for a number of problems in our society.

      S   V
The house slid into the ravine after the rain weakened the cliffs below it.

      S   V
The committee voted to reduce the homeowners' fees.

To add some variety to your writing, try opening more of your sentences with something other than the subject and verb of the main clause. Here are some possibilities.

- **Open your sentence with a subordinate clause.**

  After the rain weakened the cliffs below it, the house slid into the ravine.

- **Open your sentence with a prepositional phrase.**

  Over the past forty years, television has been blamed for a number of problems in our society.

- **Open your sentence with a verbal phrase.**

  Responding to the complaints from a majority of the owners, the committee voted to reduce the homeowners' fees. (present participial phrase)

  Concerned about the rising cost of living, the committee voted to reduce the homeowners' fees. (past participial phrase)

  To prevent people from having to sell their homes, the committee voted to reduce the homeowners' fees. (infinitive phrase)

EXERCISE

Revise the following paragraph to improve its sentence variety.

1. The story of "Rudolph, the Red-Nosed Reindeer" was created in 1939 by Robert May. 2. He worked for Montgomery Ward as an ad writer. 3. The store management wanted something special to hand out to children over Christmas. 4. They asked May to write a poem. 5. May decided upon a reindeer as the subject of his poem. 6. His four-year-old daughter helped him to select the name. 7. A store artist went to the zoo to develop reindeer sketches. 8. Johnny Marks put "Rudolph, the Red-Nosed Reindeer" to music in 1947. 9. Gene Autry recorded the song. 10. "Rudolph, the Red-Nosed Reindeer" became the second-best-selling record of all time.

APPENDIX
ANSWERS TO ODD-NUMBERED EXERCISES

Page 71

1. <u>Environmental agencies like the Environmental Protection Agency are having an impact on our neighborhood.</u>
3. <u>Auto companies like Ford and Honda are developing electrical cars because the government has set a deadline for their introduction.</u>
5. <u>The electrical cars are very quiet; therefore, they decrease noise pollution also.</u>
7. <u>Environmental laws have also caused an increase in the coyotes and raccoons in my neighborhood.</u>
9. <u>The birds in our area have increased in number and variety because pesticide use has decreased.</u>

Page 74 (Other correct answers are possible.)

1. Andrea enjoyed listening to John Coltrane, a jazz saxophonist whom she had admired for a long time.
3. She followed his career, going to see him at every opportunity.
5. Correct
7. This group included the pianist McCoy Tyner; Elvin Jones played the drums.
9. Andrea admired the songs John Coltrane wrote himself. Her special favorites were "Alabama" and "After the Rain."

Pages 76–77 (Other correct answers are possible.)

1. Recently, some older fashions and fads have returned, but they are not especially attractive ones.
3. These shoes are not just unattractive; they might even be dangerous.
5. In addition, bell bottoms have reappeared. At least when they were worn by sailors they had some practical purpose.
7. Yo-yos have also returned, and the hula hoop should reappear soon.
9. Perhaps these old fashions are popular because the year 2000 is approaching, although there might not be any specific reason for their popularity.

Pages 80–81

1. Our choice of movies has become interesting in recent years.
3. One of the most popular and expensive of disaster films has been *Titanic*.

5. Is the movie industry or today's audiences fearful because a millennium is ending?

7. In addition to these, there are disaster movies such as *Sudden Impact, Volcano,* and *Twister.*

9. Every viewer, young or old, has different reasons for seeing these films.

Page 83

1. Supposedly when Hemingway wrote his novels, he decided to compose just one hundred precise words each day.

3. My professors used to point out that he used almost no adjectives.

5. His favorite story was "Cat in the Rain," which is only about two pages long.

7. But he wrote "Cat in the Rain" convincingly from the point of view of a woman.

9. The story reveals just a few details about the couple, and we are supposed to draw inferences from those details.

Page 86

1. A few years ago my family bought Darby, an Australian Shepherd, from a breeder.

3. In Australia, dogs like Darby once herded sheep and cattle.

5. The breeder told us to keep newspapers on the laundry room floor for the first few days.

7. Within a week, our new pet could catch and return a Frisbee.

9. For fun my daughter Michelle sometimes called Darby names like "Darbaloney," "Darbinger," "Darboney," or "Miss Darby."

Page 89

1. When a person enters our town's new cybermall, he or she will be impressed by its extensive use of technology.

3. When people check out the mini-computer, they have to leave an ID like a driver's license.

5. Correct

7. Someone once told me that she loves the coffee at the Technomat.

9. The mini-computers show people who are using them what is in each store and how to get there.

Page 91 (Other correct answers are possible.)

1. General Beauregard and General Lee were discussing General Beauregard's (or General Lee's) horse.

3. General Pickett thought that a blacksmith should look at Traveller because the horse acted lame, so General Lee took Traveller to the blacksmith.

5. Because Pickett's horse looked like the one Lee had ridden at West Point, Lee began to remember his student days.

7. The report that Pickett read said that Gettysburg could be easily taken.

9. Pickett's wife talked to Lee's mother, who was worried about her son.

Pages 94–95

1. My professor and I were discussing Tony Hillerman.

3. One of the differences between her and me is that she is from the South and I am from the Southwest.

5. In fact, she knows more about the settings of Hillerman's novels than I, even though I was born in Arizona and lived in New Mexico.

7. In the novels, Chee and Leaphorn are always involving themselves in solving crimes around the Four Corners area.

9. Because she is an expert on the history of the Southwest, she knows much more than I about these customs.

Page 97

1. The psychologist told us to watch the presentation on road rage carefully.

3. While talking on a cellular phone, a man with a toy poodle in the back seat became angry with an old woman who was crossing a busy street.

5. Correct

7. Infuriated, the driver who had been rammed responded with an insulting hand gesture.

9. The English teacher drove nearly twenty miles before he pulled over.

Pages 99–100 (Other correct answers are possible.)

1. Slipping the disk into the drive, Jack watched as the icon appeared on the screen.

3. After Jack installed the program, a large question mark appeared on the screen.

5. Jack could see the outlines of a scenic mountain range as it slowly assembled on the monitor screen.

7. Confused and irritated by the computer, Tasha clicked on one icon after another.

9. Aaron smiled broadly when the computer revealed his favorite site.

Page 104

1. Originating in Greek mythology, the story of Icarus and Daedalus has been interpreted in several ways.

3. The two men gather wax and feathers, and Daedalus constructs wings for them.

5. My son first heard the story of Icarus from a waiter at the Feta Cheese Cafe, 1416 James Joyce Way, Dublin, Ireland, when he was ten years old.

7. Icarus, unfortunately, is an excitable boy, so he does not obey.

9. When Icarus gets close to the sun, the wax on his wings melts, the feathers fall off, and he perishes in the sea.

Pages 106–107

1. Enrique wanted to study classical guitar; Mary preferred to learn the clarinet.

3. Because we were completely exhausted, we all went to bed and fell asleep.

5. Correct

7. The play had finally ended; it was time to go home.

9. The Grinch hates many things about Christmas: the singing, the gift-giving, and especially the sense of joy and peace.

Pages 108–109

1. It was time to perform the annual Christmas ritual: select a tree, cut it down, haul it home, set it up, and decorate it with ornaments.

3. Last night's speaker has a strange hobby: he collects used horseshoes.

5. Mark Twain once made the following observation: "The lack of money is the root of all evil."

7. Jake could not believe it: his sister had won the state lottery.

9. According to Oscar Wilde, "Marriage is hardly a thing that one can do now and again—except in America."

Page 111

1. That is Oscar's football; he isn't using it today.

3. The principal's face turned beet red when he realized the car was ours.

5. People thought that Carla's performance wasn't as powerful as Jerry's.

7. We're going to form a study group, and you're all invited to join.

9. The two brothers' main concern was how to find a good therapist for their parents.

Page 114

1. Ovid wrote, "To be loved, be lovable."

3. Who was it who said, "All's fair in love and war"?

5. Darby also likes this quotation from La Rouchefoucald: "In jealousy there is more self-love than love."

7. Correct

9. "Ah, love," wrote the poet, "let us be true to one another."

Page 116

1. The movie Elizabeth contained many historical inaccuracies.

3. The article in Newsweek was entitled "U.S. versus Microsoft: Slower Than the Web."

5. In Shakespeare's play The Merchant of Venice, there is much discussion of a "pound of flesh."

7. Lilith is studying re-runs of the television program Frazier for her dissertation.

9. Professor Hibbard says that he teaches Robert Frost's poem "Stopping by Woods on a Snowy Evening" because of the special meter.

Page 118

1. Flo saw Aunt Beatrice on New Year's Day.

3. The film about Islamic history was produced by Warner Brothers.

5. As Carl's professor was lecturing on Paradise Lost, Carl was thinking about Christmas.

7. When I buy cookies from the Girl Scouts, I tend to overspend.

9. When my father thinks of the New York Stock Exchange, he worries about bears.

Page 120

1. Three hundred thirteen Minnesotans watched the Whippets beat the Troglodytes 15 to 14.

3. By 5:32 I had won $2.60 at the racetrack.

5. The nurses were bargaining for a 5% raise, but they were offered only 2.5%.

7. By the end of Act 5 of Hamlet, seven people have died.

9. At 10:45 Professor Hohman told us to reconsider the meaning of Chapter 43 of Tristram Shandy.

Page 126

1. Marlyle said it was all right with her if I did not follow her advice.
3. Sara was too excited to fall asleep when she lay down for her nap.
5. When he heard Johnny's excuse, the principal did not know whether to laugh or cry.
7. A green pickup sped past the school and slammed into the back of your car.
9. Thunderball led the entire race until just before the finish line, where he lost by a nose.

Pages 129–130

1. Janet could hardly believe that she had misspelled such an easy word.
3. Bald eagles are rarely seen in these mountains, and it is illegal to hunt them.
5. When he admitted how many chocolates he had eaten, everyone gasped.
7. The two attorneys decided to falsify the missing receipt.
9. In the excitement of the party, no one noticed that a theft had occurred.

Page 134

1. Jerry owns a big black cat and a tiny toy poodle.
3. The principal led the angry people into his office.
5. The person who owns the red Honda is shouting at me.
7. Whenever we go to a baseball game, my son buys a hot dog.
9. Last year I visited the Philippines for the first time.

Page 137

1. After breakfast, my uncle will read the paper.
3. The man who was standing at the corner has taken that woman's purse.
5. Did your son walk all the way home?
7. Everyone who meets that man is frightened by his violent behavior.
9. Please be quiet because I am concentrating on my homework.

Page 139

1. An ugly blue car drove down the deserted street.
3. Al picked up two tiny square dice and threw them across the table.
5. After the grueling basketball game, Jackson was completely exhausted.
7. We decided to have dinner at an expensive Chinese restaurant.
9. Correct

Pages 144–145 (Other correct answers are possible.)

1. I was stunned when I heard what he had said.
3. To lose weight, he started to attend his local gym.
5. George's mother started to cry at the funeral.
7. Although I love the beach, I know that too much sun can damage my skin.
9. Alger opened his lunch box and stared at the food in it.

Page 148 (Other correct answers are possible.)

1. After the exhausting game, Carlton slept soundly.
3. Our family is spending too much, but saving money is very difficult.
5. After our business went bankrupt, I felt completely hopeless.
7. Because she did not want to disturb her parents, Jenna was as quiet as she could be when she came home at 5:00 a.m.
9. The salesperson at the car lot thought he was being clever, but I knew exactly what he was trying to do.

Pages 151–152

1. I remember what my childhood house looked like.
3. He left the room because the television was too loud.
5. My father wants us to drive to Utah this summer.
7. We will remain seated until the show ends.
9. Today, no one should ever go hungry.

Page 154 (Other correct answers are possible.)

1. Before we leave, we need to fill the car with gas and to buy some food.
3. The skier stepped into his ski bindings, grabbed his poles, and then fell flat on his face.
5. Too much exposure to the sun can cause mild sunburn today and serious skin cancer in the future.
7. Last summer we visited relatives in Sioux Falls, gambled in Deadwood City, and water-skied on Lake Ponset.
9. The cabin disappointed Sergio because the windows were broken and the furniture was shabby.

Page 157

Answers will vary.

INDEX

A
A/an/the, 133–134
Action verbs, 151
Active voice
changing passive to, 85–86
identifying and choosing, 84
Adjectives
placing, 138–139
using present and past participles as, 139
Agreement
noun and pronoun, 87–89
subject-verb, 78–81
between verbs and pronouns, 30
And, 153
Anecdotal conclusions, 26
Anecdotal introductions, 17–18
Answers to odd-numbered exercises, 159–165
Apostrophes, 31, 110–111
to form contractions, 110
to form possessives, 110
personal pronouns and, 111
Argumentative papers, 10
Articles
cited in sample research paper, 65
finding older articles for research papers, 50–51
finding with computerized databases, 50
using in research papers, 50
on Works Cited page, 58–59
Author and page number references, 56
Authority
adding in transitions, 54
supporting ideas with references to, 22
Authors
citing multiple, 59
citing two works for same, 57, 59

B
Backing up word-processed papers, 35
Back-to-front proofreading, 31
Body paragraphs, 7, 8, 9
adding details in, 23

developing with supporting sentences, 20–21
opening with topic sentences, 20–21
relating supporting sentences to topic sentence, 22–23
Books. See also Reading
computerized card catalog searches for, 49–50
using for research papers, 49
on Works Cited page, 58
Brainstorming, 4

C
Capitalization, 117–118
Chronological development of ideas, 13
Clauses
misplaced, 96–97
as sentence openers, 156–157
using colons after complete main, 108
Clichés, 146–148
Clustering, 4–5
Collective nouns, 88
Colons, 108–109
after complete main clause, 108
spacing of, 33
Combining short sentences, 155–156
Commas, 101–104
after introductory element, 102
before coordinating conjunctions, 101
before elements in a series, 101–102
combining short sentences with coordinating conjunctions and, 155
comma splices, 75–76
setting off interrupting elements, 102–103
spacing of, 33
Commonly confused words, 121–126
Comparison/contrast development, 14
Comparisons, 93–94
Computers
citing references for Internet resources, 59–60
proofreading printed copy of work, 35
researching papers on Internet, 51
saving and backing up work, 35

Computers (*continued*)
    searching for book and articles with,
        49–50
    using grammar and style programs, 36
    using spelling checker, 35, 127
Concluding paragraphs, 7, 9, 25–26
    as part of formal paper, 7, 9
    purpose of, 25
    restating thesis idea in, 25
    tips for creating, 26
    types of, 25–26
Conjunctions
    coordinating, 155
    correlative, 153–154
    subordinate, 70
Contractions, 110
Coordinating conjunctions, 155
Correcting typographical errors, 34
Correlative conjunctions, 153–154
Cousins, N., 43–45

D
Dangling modifiers, 98–100
Dashes, 33
Decline of Neatness, The (Cousins),
        43–45
Dictionaries, 127
Direct quotations, 53
Dividing
    long paragraphs, 7
    words, 34
Documenting sources, 55–60
    with parenthetical references, 55–57
    with Works Cited page, 57–60
-*d* or -*ed* endings for past tense verbs, 82
"Dumped" quotations, 54

E
Editing, 30–31, 69–130. *See also* Revising
        papers
    agreement between verbs and pro-
        nouns, 30
    apostrophes, 31, 110–111
    capitalization, 117–118
    colons, 108–109
    commas, 101–104
    consistency in verb voice, 84–86
    correcting typographical errors, 34

    creating consistency in verb tense,
        82–83
    dangling modifiers, 98–100
    fragments and run-on sentences, 30
    fused sentences and comma splices,
        75–76
    with grammar and style software pro-
        grams, 36
    misplaced modifiers, 96–97
    numbers, 119–120
    preliminary thesis statements, 10, 12
    pronoun agreement, 87–89
    pronoun case, 92–95
    pronoun reference, 90–91
    proofreading tips, 31
    quotation marks, 112–114
    recognizing complete sentences, 69–71
    revising papers v., 27
    run-on sentences, 75–77
    semicolons, 105–107
    sentence fragments, 72–74
    spelling, 30, 127–130
    subject-verb agreement, 78–81
    titles, 115–116
    words commonly confused, 121–126
Elements in a series, 101–102
Ellipses, 33
Emphatic order, 14
Encyclopedias
    citing as reference, 59
    using in research papers, 49
English as a second language, 133–139
    a/an/the, 133–134
    placing adjectives, 138–139
    using helping verbs and main verbs,
        135–137
    using present participle and past par-
        ticiple as adjectives, 139
Essay exams, 39–41
Euphemisms, 146–148
Examples, 22
Exclamation marks, 33
Exercise answers, 159–165
Expository papers, 10–11

F
Facts, 22
Fonts for printing, 32

Formal papers. *See* Research papers; Writing
Formatting papers, 32–34
 choosing paper stock, 32
 correcting errors, 34
 dividing words, 34
 ink and fonts for printing, 32
 margins and justification, 32
 spacing and punctuation marks, 33
 titles and title pages, 32–33
 typing, 33
Freewriting, 3–4
Fused sentences, 75–76

G
General-to-specific introductions, 17
Getting started writing. *See* Starting to write
Grammar
 editing with software programs, 36
 revising in later drafts, 6
Grouping related points, 13

H
He/him, 92
Helping verbs, 135, 136–137

I
I/me, 92
In-class paper and essay exams, 39–41
 getting started, 40
 preparing for essay exams, 39
 preparing for in-class papers, 39
 writing, 41
Informal language and slang, 144
Ink and fonts for printing, 32
Internet
 citing references for, 59–60
 researching papers on, 51
Interviews
 parenthetical references for, 57
 on Works Cited page, 60
Introductory paragraphs, 16–19
 avoiding definitions and announcements in, 18–19
 drafting preliminary, 16
 as part of formal paper, 7, 8

placing thesis statement in, 11–12, 16–17
 purpose of, 16
 types of, 17–18
It, 91
Italicizing titles, 115

J
Jargon, 143
Joining ideas
 with *and* or *or*, 153–154
 combining short sentences, 155–156
Justification, 32

L
Lectures, 57
Lists
 in parallel sentences, 153
 semicolons in, 105

M
Magazines, 58
Main clauses, 69–70
Main verbs, 135–137
Margins, 32
Memorizing tricks for spelling, 127
Misplaced modifiers, 96–97
Modifiers
 dangling, 98–100
 misplaced, 96–97

N
Newspapers, 58
Noncount nouns, 133–134
Nouns
 agreement with pronouns, 87–89
 noncount, 133–134
 plural count, 133
 proper, 134
 singular count, 133
 singular pronouns and collective, 88
Numbers, 119–120
 spelling out, 119
 using numerals for, 119–120

O
Opening quotation introductions, 18
Or, 153

Organizing ideas, 13–14
after starting paper, 6
allowing organization to change as you
write, 15
in chronological order, 13
in comparison/contrast order, 14
deciding if you have enough material,
13
in emphatic order, 14
grouping related points, 13
in parallel order, 14–15
point-by-point, 14
for research papers, 52–53
in spatial order, 13
Outlining
main and supportive ideas, 43
writing the first draft and, 52–53
Overly formal language and jargon, 143

P
Page number only references, 55–56
Paired pronouns, 93
Pamphlets, 60
Paper stock, 32
Paper topics, 3–6. *See also* Starting to write
brainstorming, 4
choosing for research papers, 48
clustering, 4–5
doing introduction later, 6
focusing on grammar, spelling, and
punctuation later, 6
freewriting, 3–4
organizing ideas later, 6
starting writing, 5
talking to other people about topic, 5
Paragraphs. *See also* Body paragraphs;
Introductory paragraphs
adding details in, 23
body, 7, 8, 9
concluding, 7, 9, 25–26
dividing long, 7
improving transitions between, 28
introductory, 7, 8, 16–19
opening body paragraphs with topic
sentences, 20–21
placing topic sentences in, 20
relating supporting sentences to topic
sentence, 22–23
strengthening choppy, 7

thesis statement in introductory, 11–12,
16–17
varying sentence length and structure,
29
writing introductory, 16–19
writing longer, 24
Parallel organization of ideas, 14–15
Parallel sentences
items in a list in, 153
items joined with correlative conjunctions, 153–154
joining ideas with *and* or *or*, 153
Paraphrases
of quotations, 53, 112
using transitions with, 54
Parenthetical references, 55–57
for lectures or interviews, 57
with page number only, 55–56
punctuating, 56
in sample research paper, 61, 62, 63,
64
secondhand quotations in, 56–57
with title and page number, 56
for two works with same author, 57, 59
types of, 55
using author and page number, 56
Passive voice
changing to active voice, 85–86
identifying and choosing, 84–85
Past tense verbs
-d or *-ed* endings for, 82
shifting to present tense, 82
Periods, 33
Personalizing words and style in
summaries, 47
Phrases
misplaced, 96–97
using as sentence openers, 156–157
Plagiarism, 54
Plural count nouns, 133
Point-by-point for organizing ideas, 14
Possessives, 110
Predictions in conclusion, 26
Present tense verbs
shifting to past tense, 82
using when discussing writing, 83
Printing papers
ink and fonts for, 32
proofreading after, 31

Pronouns
  agreement between nouns and, 87–89
  agreement between verbs and, 30
  apostrophes and personal, 111
  avoiding apostrophes with personal, 111
  case of, 92–95
  collective nouns and singular, 88
  in comparisons, 93–94
  paired, 93
  pronoun reference, 90–91
  sexist language and, 88
  singular v. plural, 87–88
  use of *you*, 87
  using *I*/*me*, *he*/*him*, *she*/*her*, and *they*/*them*, 92
  using *-self*/*-selves*, 94
  using *who* and *whom*, 93
Proofreading, 31
  correcting typographical errors, 34
  printed copy of paper, 35
Proper nouns, 134
Punctuation
  adding later in later drafts, 6
  apostrophes, 31, 110–111
  colons, 33, 108–109
  commas, 33, 75–76, 101–104
  ellipses, 33
  exclamation marks, 33
  in parenthetical references, 56
  periods, 33
  quotation marks, 53, 54, 112–114
  semicolons, 33, 105–107

Q
Question marks, 33
Quotation marks, 112–114. *See also* Quotations
  around exact words, 112
  for long quotations, 113
  paraphrasing and, 53, 112
  punctuation at end of quotations, 113
  for quotations within quotations, 114
  transitions and punctuation before, 54, 112–113
Quotations. *See also* Quotation marks
  in conclusions, 26
  direct, 53
  integrating into paper, 54, 112–113
  long, 113
  opening introductions using, 18
  paraphrasing, 53, 112
  secondhand, 56–57
  within quotations, 114

R
Radio on Works Cited page, 60
Reading, 42–45
  annotating while, 42–43
  outlining main and supportive ideas, 43
  as preparation for writing summaries, 46
  sample annotated reading selection, 43–45
  steps before, 42
  underline while, 42
  writing response to, 43
Recommendation conclusions, 26
References. *See* Parenthetical references; Works Cited page
Relative pronouns, 70
Repetitious writing, 149–150
Research papers, 48–65. *See also* Paper topics; Writing
  avoiding plagiarism, 54
  choosing topics for, 48
  developing thesis for, 48–49
  example of entries on Work Cited page, 58–60
  finding older articles for, 50–51
  guidelines for Works Cited page, 57
  integrating sources into paper, 53–54
  parenthetical references in, 55–56, 57, 59
  researching topics, 49
  research resources for, 51
  sample research paper, 61–65
  searching for books with computerized catalog systems, 49–50
  taking notes for, 51–52
  using articles for, 50
  using books for, 49
  using computerized databases for articles, 50
  using encyclopedias and other references, 49
  using the Internet for, 51
  writing the first draft, 52–53

Reviewers, having paper proofread by, 31
Revising papers, 27–29. *See also* Editing
 checking the organization, 27
 clarifying topic sentences, 27
 developing supporting material, 28
 editing v. revising, 27
 improving transitions, 28
 improving word choice, 29
 refining thesis, 12, 27
 varying sentence length and structure,
  29
Run-on sentences, 75–77
 editing, 30
 fused sentences and comma splices,
  75–76

S
Sample annotated reading selection,
 43–45
Sample research paper, 61–65
Sample summary, 47
Saving work as you go, 35
Searching for books and articles with computerized systems, 49–50
-self/-selves pronouns, 94
Semicolons, 105–107
 combining short sentences with, 155
 joining main clauses, 105
 in lists, 105
 spacing of, 33
 when to avoid, 106
Sentence fragments
 editing, 30
 types of, 72–73
Sentences. *See also* Topic sentences
 combining short, 155–156
 developing topic sentences, 20–21
 editing fragments and run-on sentences,
  30
 improving transition, 28
 improving word choice in, 29
 opening with clauses and phrases,
  156–157
 parallel, 153–154
 recognizing and fixing sentence fragments, 72–74
 recognizing complete, 69–71
 subject-verb agreement, 78–81
 supporting, 22–24

varying length and structure of, 29
 varying sentence length and structure,
  155–157
She/her, 92
Singular count nouns, 133
Singular v. plural pronouns, 87–88
Slang, 144
Spacing, 33
Spatial development for organizing ideas,
 13
Special assignments, 39–65
 in-class paper and essay exams, 39–41
 reading actively and accurately, 42–45
 writing summaries, 46–47
Spelling, 30, 127–130
 basic rules for, 127–129
 checking after initial draft, 6
 checking dictionary for, 127
 numbers out, 119
 tricks for remembering, 127
 using spelling checker, 35, 127
Starting to write, 3–6
 clustering, 4–5
 freewriting, 3–4
 with in-class paper and essay exams,
  39–40
 organizing ideas after, 6
 summaries, 46
 thinking on paper, 5
Strengthening choppy paragraphs, 7
Structure of thesis statement, 11
Style in writing, 143–157. *See also* Writing
 avoiding clichés and euphemisms, 146–
  148
 eliminating redundancies, 149–150
 informal language and slang, 144
 overly formal language and jargon, 143
 parallel sentence structure, 153–155
 replacing roundabout phrases, 150
 using action verbs, 151
 varying sentence length and structure,
  155–157
Subject-verb agreement, 78–81
Subordinate clauses, 70
 combining short sentences with, 156
 using who and whom with, 93
Subordinate conjunctions, 70
Summaries
 characteristics of, 46

integrating ideas into research papers with, 53
preparing to write, 46
sample summary, 47
of supporting points in thesis statements, 11
using own words and style in, 47
writing, 46
Summary conclusions, 25
Supporting sentences, 22–24
adding details with, 23
developing longer paragraph, 24
relating to topic sentence, 22–23
types of support for ideas, 22

T
Taking notes, 51–52
Talking to others about topics, 5
Television, on Works Cited page, 60
Tense
creating consistency in verb, 82–83
shifting, 82
That, 90–91
The, 133–134
Thesis statements, 10–12
for argumentative papers, 10
developing, 48–49
editing, 10, 12
for expository papers, 10–11
placing in introduction, 11–12, 16–17
refining, 27
restating in conclusion, 25
revising, 12, 27
structure of, 11
summarizing points in, 11
supporting, 20–21
writing preliminary, 10
They/them, 92
This, 90
Title and page number references, 56
Titles, 115–116
formatting titles and title pages, 32–33
of longer works, 115
of own paper, 115
of shorter works, 115
To be verbs, 151
Topics. See Paper topics
Topic sentences, 20–21
as beginning of paragraph, 20

revising and clarifying, 27
in sample research paper, 61, 62, 63
supporting examples for, 22–23
supporting thesis statement, 20–21
writing effective, 21
writing preliminary, 20
Transitions
before quotation marks, 112–113
improving, 28
integrating quotations with, 54
in sample research paper, 61, 62, 63
Typing papers
on computer, 35
correcting typographical errors, 34
formatting guidelines, 33

U
Underlining titles, 115

V
Varying sentence length and structure, 155–157
Verbs, 135–137
agreement between pronouns and, 30
combining helping and main, 136–137
consistency in voice, 84–86
creating consistency in tense, 82–83
helping, 135
identifying and choosing active voice, 84
main, 135–136
subject-verb agreement, 78–81
using action, 151
Video or audio recordings on Works Cited page, 60

W
Which, 90
Who/whom, 93
Words
avoiding clichés and euphemisms, 146–148
commonly confused, 121–126
dividing, 34
editing redundant, 149–150
improving word choice, 29
informal language and slang, 144
memorizing tricks for spelling, 127

Words (*continued*)
  misplaced, 96
  overly formal language and jargon, 143
Works Cited page
  example of entries on, 58–60
  guidelines for, 57
  sample, 65
  taking notes for, 51–52
Writing, 3–36. *See also* Research papers;
    Starting to write; Thesis statements
  about reading topics, 43
  allowing flexible organization as you
    write, 15
  avoiding plagiarism, 54
  beginning to write, 3–6, 39–40
  clichés and euphemisms in, 146–148
  clustering, 4–5
  on computer, 35, 127
  cutting needless repetitions, 149–150
  deciding if you have enough material,
    13
  developing supporting material, 11,
    22–24, 28

  discussing in present tense, 83
  dividing long paragraphs, 7
  editing, 30–31
  first draft of research paper, 52–53
  formatting papers, 32–34
  informal language and slang, 144
  introductory paragraphs, 16–19
  organizing ideas, 13–15
  overly formal language and jargon, 143
  parallel sentence structure, 153–155
  revising, 27–29
  summaries, 46
  thesis statements, 10–12
  topic sentences, 20–23, 27, 61, 62, 63
  using action verbs, 151
  using paragraphs, 7–9
  varying sentence length and structure,
    155–157
  writing longer paragraphs, 24

Y
You, 87